Navigating Autism

"Takiwātanga"

In their own space and time

Navigating Autism
One child's journey

Shae Talalelei

Learning Exceptionalities Press
Tacoma, WA

First published 2024

by Learning Exceptionalities Press
Tacoma, WA

© Shae Talalelei

All rights reserved. No part of this book may be reprinted or reproduced or utilized in any form or by any electronic, mechanical, or other means, now known or hereafter invented, including photocopying and recording, or in any information storage retrieval system, without permission in writing from the publisher.

Trademark notice: Product or corporate names may be trademarks or registered trademarks and are used only for identification and explanation without intent to infringe.

Library of Congress Control Number:

ISBN 978-1-7353333-4-2 (pbk)
ISBN 978-1-7353333-5-9 (ebk)

Typeset in Palatino linotype
by Monotype Typography, Inc

Cover illustration by Iconic_Agnecy (Fivver)

Book design by Shae Talalelei

Printed and bound by IngramSpark.

Dedicated

To my wonderful sons,

You are the sunshine that lights up my life. Everything I do, I do for you. You bring me immense joy and endless love, and I would go to the ends of the Earth to make you happy. You make me proud every day, and this book is a result of how you inspire me to be the best person I can be. You are my little heroes.

To my loving husband,

You are my rock and my best friend. Our sons are so lucky to have you as their father. Your belief in them and your unwavering support for their happiness mean the world to us. I see and appreciate every sacrifice you've made. This book was made possible with your incredible help, and I'm deeply thankful.

To my dear family,

You are my everything. Through thick and thin, you've stood by us and fought alongside us for our sons' well-being. Your presence brings peace to our lives and strength to our journey, and we couldn't do this journey without you. There were moments when my world grew so dark that I couldn't find my path, yet you consistently emerged as guiding lights, illuminating my way. Through your unwavering presence and support, you've been my constant strength, helping me navigate even the toughest of times. Your role in this journey is immeasurable, and I am forever grateful for your unwavering love and light.

To my amazing friends,

In a world where good friends can be hard to find, we struck gold with all of you. Your love and support have made our lives feel normal even in the toughest times. You've been our anchor, and this book is as much a product of your care as it is of our own determination. Thank you from the bottom of our hearts.

Dr. John Inman and Sana Tariq

Who taught, me how to navigate a world that was never designed for my child, so I could conquer challenges and shape the world he deserves.

Laura, Adriana, Taylor, and Cindy

To all those who stood by my side and provided unwavering support throughout this journey, you serve as my beacon of light when the path grows dim.

Table of Contents

Dedicated 7

Table of Contents 9

Acknowledgments xv

Introduction 1

The Diagnosis 1

Introduction 1

Therapy 7

Interpreting Evaluation Results 7

Insurance Insights 15

Finance 23

Financial Considerations 23

Education 27

Legal Aspects 36

Developmental Preschool Explained 38

Charter schools, Public schools, Private schools, and Cooperative schools 46

Parent and School Responsibilities: 54

Finding a Specialist 59

Finding Doctors Specializing in Autism 59

Outings 63

    Places 63

    Creating your safe group 66

    Concerns to Address 68

    Things to Want and Expect 69

    Accommodations and Inclusivity 70

    Day trips, road trips and flying what to pack, expect and prepare. 75

Flying 79

    Social Stories 82

Autism Glossary 91

Admirable Professionals 97

    Eastside Therapy Services 98

    Speech For Success, PLLC 100

    Columbia Virtual Academy 103

    Dr. John Inman 108

    Sana Tariq 109

    Learning To Play 110

Words from the Author 114

Acknowledgments

I would like to express my deepest gratitude to Dr. John Inman, whose unwavering support and guidance were instrumental in the creation of my first book. Dr. Inman's encouragement and refusal to let me give up served as a constant source of inspiration. Having read his remarkable book 'Twice Exceptional", I am truly grateful for the profound impact it had on my journey as a writer.

A special acknowledgment goes to the wonderful staff and educators at Columbia Virtual Academy. Your dedication to helping all students, regardless of abilities and inabilities, has proven that there are educators who go above and beyond. You are paving a way that I hope many other schools follow.

I extend my heartfelt thanks to the therapists who work with sheer dedication to help set up these wonderful gifted little ones for a world that isn't always set up for them. Your commitment to making a difference is truly commendable.

Lastly, but most importantly, I want to express my gratitude to the family and friends who understood and stood by me through thick and thin. Your unwavering support has been my anchor, and I am profoundly thankful for each one of you. Together, we are making a difference in the lives of these exceptional individuals."

Introduction

I am a mother of a child with Autism, much like many of you who have picked up this book, I was inundated with feelings of overwhelm as I embarked on this journey with my son. Back then, I possessed only a fraction of the knowledge I now hold. The contents of this book reflect my personal journey and the experiences I've encountered here in Washington State. As I continue to learn and my son grows, I hope to pen another book to share my evolving insights.

My aspiration is that this guide will serve as a source of assistance, helping to alleviate any weight you may be carrying following your diagnosis. I want you to recognize that you're not alone in your feelings; it's okay to experience sadness or to yearn for a respite. After all, you're a human being, not an emotionless machine. As a parent or caregiver, you're already doing everything in your capacity to support someone you hold dear. My aim is to furnish you with the information I wish I had when I first set foot on this path.

You possess the capability, the resilience of a warrior, and the assurance that you're not alone in this journey. Remember, you are enough. This path may be challenging, but with each chapter you and your child navigate, you emerge stronger and more self-assured.

The Diagnosis

Introduction

Receiving a diagnosis of autism can be a monumental challenge to overcome. At this point, you'll gain insights into where your child stands on the autism spectrum and whether they might exhibit other developmental delays linked to autism, such as speech Apraxia. It's important to note that Apraxia isn't inherently tied to autism, and vice versa. I mention it because discovering additional aspects beyond autism during diagnosis is common. Although this might seem overwhelming, please be aware that service providers in our state are available to address all facets of your child's needs that accompany their autism journey. You may also uncover the remarkable gifts your child possesses.

Identifying Signs

From my personal experience, I didn't recognize my son's autism until he reached around 3 years old. However, at 18 months, certain behaviors raised concerns for me that might not have caught the attention of others. For instance, he exhibited a regression in speech, engaged in less one-on-one play and interaction with peers, displayed fixation on one toy at a time, and demonstrated an inclination to sort or line up toys by color, shape, or size.

2 The Diagnosis

Additionally, he exhibited remarkable gifts, having memorized both lowercase and uppercase letters of the American alphabet, could count forward and backward to 20, and even knew the Arabic alphabet by age 2. By age 3, he was already delving into addition. Seeking guidance, I consulted our pediatrician who promptly provided a referral—an essential step that all pediatricians should take, regardless of whether they suspect autism. Pediatricians are trained in general medicine, not autism diagnosis, which necessitates referring to specialists with the expertise to make such assessments. It's worth noting that some parents have encountered resistance when requesting referrals or have been told to wait. Remember that you're entitled to advocate for your child's needs and secure a referral from a willing professional. Early diagnosis is beneficial, so trust your instincts. It is important to remember that children on the spectrum often demonstrate exceptional gifts, displaying unique talents and strengths that contribute to their individuality and make valuable contributions to various aspects of life.

Here's a list of general signs to be aware of. Keep in mind that every child with autism is unique, and not all may display these signs. As the saying goes, "When you've met one person with autism, you've met one person with autism." Each individual's experience is distinct, so the signs might vary:

- Unresponsiveness to their name
- Regression in speech
- Lack of eye contact
- Preference for solitude and independent play
- Fixation on specific items or topics
- Limited social interest

- Engaging in repetitive behaviors such as hand-flapping or walking on toes

For more comprehensive information, consider referring to the National Autism Association's free downloadable PDF resource, which I strongly recommend. I'll provide contact details and site information at the end of this book.

The Diagnosis Process and Referral

Obtaining a referral, as mentioned earlier, can either be straightforward or challenging. If your doctor hesitates, articulate the necessity for an early intervention due to your child's potential autism diagnosis. Should they remain unyielding, consider seeking another pediatrician, ensuring you research them beforehand. If urgency demands, you can consult a specialist without a referral, albeit at your own cost. However, some places offer sliding scale fees, payment plans, and assistance. After securing a referral from your pediatrician, consider requesting multiple referrals to various locations in your area to mitigate potential waitlist delays. Below, I've compiled a list of personally recommended organizations here in the Seattle area. Further details about these institutions can be found at the conclusion of this book. If you reside outside of Seattle of Washington state, examine reviews for the centers you are contemplating for your child and inquire about their study methodologies and process. For instance, inquire about the types of assessments they conduct, the duration of sessions, and any personalized approaches they employ to cater to individual needs.

- Seattle Children's Autism Center
- UW Autism Center
- Caravel Autism Health (Imagine Behavior)

Expectations During the Evaluation

Evaluations can span from 1 to 2 hours. The psychologist will invite you and your child into a room to perform various assessments, evaluating speech, behavior, sensory sensitivities, and needs. You might be asked to complete a questionnaire addressing these aspects to compare your observations with theirs. Here are a few tips for a smoother experience:

- Schedule an early morning evaluation; children often show clearer signs in the morning.
- Research clinic reviews to gauge the appropriateness of the facility.
- Ensure you're permitted to be present during the evaluation. Your presence can be reassuring.
- Pack their favorite snacks, toys, or calming tools to soothe them post-evaluation.

Questions for the Psychologist

- What areas will you assess?
- How long does the assessment typically take?
- Will my child be allowed breaks?
- I prefer a natural and holistic approach; is that your methodology?
- Can I contact you after receiving the results?
- How long until I receive the evaluation outcomes?

Post-Evaluation Concerns

Following the evaluation, you'll converse with the evaluating physician. While this may feel intimidating, remember that everything will be alright. Breathe deeply, enjoy your coffee or tea, and understand that regardless of what you learn, support communities and resources are available to guide you through this journey.

Therapy

Interpreting Evaluation Results

Upon reviewing your child's evaluation, you will gain insights into observed developmental delays and their severity. It's important to remember that these assessments can change over time, as your child continues to grow and develop. The evaluation does not define them; rather, it guides us toward areas that might need more nurturing. You'll receive a list of recommended services and the suggested number of weekly hours for each. Common services include:

Speech Therapist (Speech-Language Pathologist - SLP): Speech therapists work with individuals who have difficulties with communication, language, speech, and social communication.

- Expressive Language: A speech therapist might work with a child who has limited verbal communication skills to help them express their needs, wants, and feelings using words or other communication tools.

- Receptive Language: They might assist in improving a child's ability to understand and follow instructions or respond appropriately to questions.

- Social Communication: For individuals who struggle with social interactions, a speech therapist might teach skills such as maintaining eye contact, taking turns in conversations, and understanding nonverbal cues.
- Assessing communication skills and identifying areas of need.
- Developing strategies to improve speech and language skills, including expressive and receptive language, articulation, and social communication.
- Teaching alternative communication methods like sign language or augmentative and alternative communication (AAC) devices.
- Enhancing social interaction skills and conversational abilities.

Occupational Therapist (OT): Occupational therapists focus on enhancing an individual's ability to perform daily activities and improve their overall quality of life.

- Sensory Integration: An occupational therapist might help a child who is sensitive to sensory stimuli, such as touch or noise, learn to tolerate and process sensory input more effectively.
- Fine Motor Skills: They might work with a child to improve skills like handwriting, using utensils, or manipulating small objects.
- Self-Care: An OT could assist an individual in developing skills necessary for activities of daily living, like getting dressed, brushing teeth, and tying shoelaces.
- Assess sensory processing and sensory integration challenges.

- Develop interventions to improve fine and gross motor skills, coordination, and balance.
- Address difficulties with self-care tasks, like dressing, grooming, and feeding.
- Help individuals manage sensory sensitivities and develop coping strategies.

Applied Behavior Analysis Therapist (ABA): is a structured approach to behavior modification and skill development. ABA therapists use evidence-based techniques to address behavior challenges and teach new skills to individuals with autism.

- Communication Skills: ABA therapists might use discrete trial teaching to help a child learn to request items, express preferences, or engage in basic conversation.
- Behavior Management: They could work on reducing problem behaviors such as tantrums or self-injury by implementing strategies like positive reinforcement and teaching alternative behaviors.
- Skill Acquisition: ABA therapists might teach a child academic skill like reading or math, self-help skills like using a fork or buttoning a shirt, and social skills like greeting others or sharing toys.
- Conduct assessments to identify problem behaviors and skill deficits.
- Develop personalized behavior intervention plans to target challenging behaviors and encourage positive behaviors.
- Use reinforcement strategies to shape desired behaviors and skills.

- Teach a wide range of skills, including communication, social, academic, and daily living skills.

Physical Therapist (PT): Focus on improving mobility, coordination, strength, and overall physical function. PTs address motor challenges that can affect movement and independence.

- Gross Motor Skills: A physical therapist could help a child with coordination difficulties learn to ride a bike, throw and catch a ball, or jump with both feet.
- Balance and Core Strength: They might work on improving a child's balance and core strength through activities like walking on balance beams, standing on one leg, or doing exercises on a stability ball.
- Mobility: For a child who has difficulty with walking or running, a PT might focus on exercises to improve overall mobility and increase endurance.
- Assess motor skills, balance, and coordination.
- Develop interventions to improve gross motor skills and mobility.
- Address difficulties with posture, gait, and physical endurance.
- Enhance physical fitness and overall well-being.

It's important to note that these examples are just a small glimpse into the wide range of skills and challenges that these therapists address. Each therapy plan is highly individualized, based on the person's strengths, needs, and goals. Collaborating with a team of therapists ensures a holistic approach to supporting individuals with autism in various areas of their development.

Organizing with a Binder

Now that the challenging steps are behind you—evaluation is complete, and therapists are secured—it's time to create a binder. This binder will be an invaluable tool to track your child's progress and facilitate the process of crafting an Individualized Education Plan (IEP) and a 504 plan when they start school.

Begin with a 3" binder and purchase some tabbed dividers. Here's what to include:

- Section One:
    - Copies of your referrals.

- Section Two:
    - All evaluations and any relevant emails exchanged with the evaluator. Email communications might contain valuable information.

- Section Three:
    - Evaluation copy from the speech therapists and progress reports. Create subsections if you switch clinics or therapists within a service type.

Therapy

- Section Four:
    - Evaluation copy from the occupational therapists and their progress reports. Create subsections if you switch clinics or therapists within a service type.

- Section Five:
    - Evaluation copy from the physical therapist and their progress reports. Create subsections if you switch clinics or therapists within a service type.

- Section Six:
    - Evaluation copy from the ABA providers and their progress report. Create subsections if you switch clinics or therapists within a service type.

- Section Seven:
    - Evaluation from your child's school psychologist once they begin school.
    - Copy of your individual education plan (IEP), both draft and final versions.
    - Copy of your parent concern letter (a sample will be attached for your reference).
    - Copy of staff contact information, including special education teacher, occupational therapist, physical therapist, principal, psychologist, and advocate if applicable.
    - Any relevant emails between you and the school regarding your child.
    - For therapists or schools that change, create new subsections or sections accordingly.

- Section Eight: Beneficial resources, such as:
    - Financial services.
    - Notes and key takeaways.
    - Helpful books.
    - Useful YouTube videos.
    - Social group lists.

Include any resources you find valuable and that you can refer to whenever needed.

Navigating a Waitlist

If you find yourself in a situation where immediate access to services isn't possible, don't be disheartened. There's plenty you can do while on a waitlist. I was once in a similar situation with my child on waitlists for every service. Here's how I managed:

YouTube offers valuable resources for speech, occupational, and physical therapy. Additionally, Coursera provides free tuition for various special needs classes. Here are some courses I found beneficial:

- "Managing ADHD, Autism, Learning Disabilities, and Concussion in School."
- "Providing Social, Emotional, Behavioral, and Specialist Education Services in School."
- "ADHD: Everyday Strategies for Elementary Students"

I also recommend the following YouTube channels:

- Coming Home to Autism
- Walkie Talkie Speech Therapy

14   Therapy

- Speech for Success

Consider exploring relevant books on Amazon:

- "Autism Spectrum Disorder in the Inclusive Classroom, 2nd edition" by Barbara L Boroson
- "Parenting a Child with Autism Spectrum Disorder" by Albert Knapp PsyD BCBA-D RPT-S
- "The Reason I Jump: The Inner Voice of a Thirteen-Year-Old Boy with Autism" by Naoki Higashida, KA Yoshida, and David Mitchell
- "Twice-Exceptional Children Are Gifts: Developing the Talents of 2e Children" by John Inman
- "Ten Things Every Child with Autism Wishes You Knew (Revised and Updated)" by Ellen Notbohm
- "Uniquely Human: A Different Way of Seeing Autism."

Podcasts can be another valuable resource:

- On-Time Autism Intervention Podcast: Ashley Penney and Jessica Greenson
- All Autism Talk
- Parenting Autism: Chris and Sandy Colter
- Autism Helper Podcast: The Autism Helper
- Autism Outreach: Rose Griffin

Insurance Insights

Dealing with insurance can be challenging. Keep copies of all referrals your doctor submits, as some insurance companies may request them. Medical supplies like diapers, pee pads, gloves, and wipes are covered by United Health and Apple Health. AAC devices might also be covered, so consider referrals from your doctor and speech and language pathologist. It's crucial to communicate with your provider to clarify what is covered and what is not. For example, inquire about specific medical services or specialized treatment to ensure you have a comprehensive understanding of your coverage.

For affordable healthcare options, in Washington state you can find information with Washington Health Plan Finder: www.wahealthplanfinder.org. If you're seeking services in your specific state, I recommend reaching out to your government official website or contacting someone in social services for guidance. Another valuable resource is Autism Speaks, which provides nationwide information. This route is particularly suggested for comprehensive and reliable information.

If you have multiple insurance plans, you can utilize your secondary insurance to cover out-of-pocket costs. Inform therapy services and medical providers about your primary and secondary insurance to avoid issues.

Applying for Disability

In Washington state, applying for disability services for a child with autism involves navigating a process that can provide valuable support but also comes with its own set of pros and cons. Here's a general overview of how to apply for disability services, along with some potential advantages and disadvantages:

Applying for Disability Services for a Child with Autism in Washington:

Step 1: Evaluation and Diagnosis:

Before applying for disability services, ensure your child has a formal diagnosis of autism from a qualified medical professional or psychologist. This diagnosis will serve as a foundation for your application.

Step 2: Eligibility Determination:

To determine eligibility for disability services, you'll need to contact the Department of Social and Health Services (DSHS) in Washington state. Specifically, you'll want to connect with the Developmental Disabilities Administration (DDA), which provides services for individuals with developmental disabilities, including autism.

- Apply for Services: You can apply for DDA services by contacting your local DDA office or applying online through the Washington State DSHS website.
- Submit Documentation: You'll need to provide documentation of your child's diagnosis, medical records, and information about their functional limitations to support your application.

- Assessment: DDA will review your application and may conduct an assessment to determine your child's eligibility for services.

- Eligibility Determination: If your child is deemed eligible, you'll work with DDA to create an Individual Support Plan (ISP) outlining the services and supports your child will receive.

Pros of Applying for Disability Services

Access to Support: Disability services can provide access to therapies, interventions, and supports that can significantly improve your child's development, communication, and overall quality of life.

Financial Assistance: Some disability services may come with financial support, including Medicaid coverage that can help offset the costs of medical treatments and therapies.

Education and Training: Disability services often include resources, training, and educational opportunities for parents, caregivers, and families to better understand and support their child's needs.

Individualized Plans: Services are tailored to your child's specific needs, helping them reach their potential and achieve developmental milestones.

Cons of Applying for Disability Services

- Application Process: The application process for disability services can be complex, requiring documentation and assessments that might be time-consuming and stressful.

- Waiting Lists: Depending on the availability of services and resources, there might be waiting lists for certain programs, delaying your child's access to support.

- Privacy Concerns: Applying for disability services may involve sharing sensitive medical and personal information, which some families might find uncomfortable.

- Stigma: There can be a stigma associated with receiving disability services, and some families might be concerned about the perception from others.

- Limited Services: While services can be beneficial, they might not always cover all the necessary therapies or interventions your child needs.

- Adaptation Period: It can take time for both your child and family to adapt to new services, routines, and interventions.

Ultimately, the decision to apply for disability services for a child with autism in Washington should be based on careful consideration of your child's needs, your family's circumstances, and the available resources. It's recommended to reach out to support organizations, advocacy groups, and professionals in the field of autism to gather more specific information and guidance tailored to your situation.

Legal Resources

There are resources for free legal aid and support for families with children with special needs in Washington. These resources can help families navigate legal issues related to education, disability rights, and other matters. Here are some organizations and programs that offer free legal assistance in Washington for families with children with special needs:

Disability Rights Washington (DRW): DRW is a protection and advocacy agency that offers free legal services and advocacy for individuals with disabilities, including children with special needs. They can assist with issues related to education, access to services, and disability rights.

Northwest Justice Project (NJP): NJP provides free civil legal assistance to low-income individuals and families in Washington. They can help with legal issues related to housing, education, public benefits, and more.

Special Education Advocacy Center (SEAC): SEAC provides information, training, and advocacy to parents of children with disabilities. While they might not provide direct legal representation, they can offer guidance on special education rights and processes.

Washington LawHelp: This online resource offers legal information, self-help resources, and referrals to legal aid organizations that can assist families with legal issues, including those related to special education and disability rights.

Pro Bono Services and Legal Clinics: Various legal aid organizations and law firms in Washington offer pro bono (free) legal services and clinics for families in need. These clinics might cover a range of legal issues, including those related to special needs.

Local Parent Advocacy Organizations: Many local parent advocacy groups and disability support organizations can provide information about legal resources available in your area.

School District Special Education Departments: School districts are required to provide information to parents about their child's special education rights. If you have concerns about your child's education, you can start by reaching out to the special education department in your school district.

When seeking free legal aid, it's a good idea to research and contact these organizations directly to inquire about their services and availability. Keep in mind that while these organizations can offer guidance and support, they might not always be able to provide direct legal representation in every case. If you're facing complex legal issues, consulting with an attorney who specializes in special education law or disability rights can be beneficial.

Disability Application

When you're ready to apply for disability, you want to be very careful and make sure you have everything you need. I would suggest going over the application at least 3 times. They will deny you for the smallest thing and you will have to do the application again and or appeal. Here is a checklist of what you will need:

Your child's information:

☐ Names and contact information for their doctors

☐ Names and contact information for ALL hospitals and/or clinics they have been treated at. (Full names/title)

☐ Any medical tests they have received for example: Neurologist, psychologist, therapist.

☐ Any medications that they take for their disability. Provide a copy of the prescription, referrals and make sure everything is spelt correctly.

☐ They will want you to grant permission to access your child's medical records You may have to submit a release form that allows them access, usually be in the application.

☐ Your social security numbers. (Both parents if both are caring for the child)

☐ Your child's social security number.

☐ Place of birth: city, state, county, country.

☐ Paystubs, tax return, unemployment records

☐ Stocks/Dividends/Pension/Retirement funds/Bonds

☐ Alimony/Child Support

☐ Bank account statements

☐ Any loan statements: car, home, etc.

☐ Trust funds/Life Insurance

☐ Rental agreement/Mortgage payment

☐ You may have to provide your landlords information if you are renting.

☐ Names and birthdates of all who live in your household.

If you need help or more information you can call them directly but expect long wait times. I would suggest calling them as soon as they open.

Finance

Financial Considerations

Several organizations offer additional assistance, although availability isn't guaranteed as their funding might be limited to specific counties. Below is a list of organizations you can reach out to.

Bens Fund: www.bensfund.org:

Established locally in 2012 by Seahawks General Manager John Schneider and his wife Traci, Bens Fund provides financial support for families and individuals with Autism. They cover a range of expenses including medical bills, supplies, equipment, and therapy services. Check out their website for more details.

The Arc "Autism Now": www.autismnow.org:

The Arc is a comprehensive resource, not just for financial assistance, but also for a wealth of other support. While they offer an array of services, their funding might be limited to specific areas. Reach out to them for more information.

24 Finance

Autism Speaks: www.autismspeaks.org:

Autism Speaks is a well-known resource offering support groups, financial assistance, advocacy resources, and more. They are a hub for a wide range of resources and information.

Washington Autism Alliance: www.washingtonautismalliance.org:

While I haven't personally used the services of the Washington Autism Alliance, it comes highly recommended by people in my network. Similar to Autism Speaks, they provide information and resources for organizations that offer assistance.

Understanding Costs

The financial implications of having a child with Autism can be surprising, according to Autism Speaks:

- Autism can cost around $60,000 annually during childhood, primarily attributed to special services and lost wages due to increased parental demands. Costs tend to rise with intellectual disability.
- Mothers of children with ASD, often serving as case managers and advocates, are less likely to work outside the home. On average, they work fewer hours and earn less compared to mothers of children without health limitations or other disabilities.

Before our son's diagnosis, both my husband and I were employed. Following the diagnosis, we decided that I would leave my career. We based this decision on factors such as income, insurance coverage, emotional readiness, and job stability. We also made adjustments to our lifestyle, some of which may resonate with you:

- Seeking more affordable housing
- Transitioning from two cars to one reliable vehicle
- Reducing dining out and cooking at home
- Brewing coffee at home
- Cutting back on unnecessary expenses
- Clothing
- Personal care
- Cable (kept internet only)
- Expensive vacations
- Gym memberships
- Premium brands (opted for generic)

These changes helped us save, although they were temporary. Occasionally, we treated ourselves while also adhering to a cash-based budget system to prevent exceeding our allowances.

We also revisited roles and responsibilities, dividing tasks like cooking and cleaning. This arrangement evolved over time, reflecting our adjustment to this new chapter. Communication is crucial. If you're navigating this journey solo, consider the option of a caregiver coming to your home; this could potentially be covered by insurance. Additionally, there's a wealth of support groups available, including the On-Time with Autism Intervention Program (OTAI) through the University of Washington: www.depts.washington.edu/uwautism/resources/on-time-autism-intervention/.

Education

The primary aspiration of all parents, whether their child has Autism or not, is to provide them with the finest education possible. Yet, this goal takes on heightened significance and brings its own set of concerns when raising a child with special needs. You might be pondering:

- Will the school offer my child a suitable education, or will they lag behind?
- Is there a risk of harm to my child?
- Will my child be segregated from peers without disabilities?
- Can I expect my child to be treated respectfully?
- Will they display patience toward my child?
- Are they willing to accommodate my child's academic, emotional, mental, and physical needs?
- Will they provide essential services like speech therapy, occupational therapy, and physical therapy?

Navigating the realm of education and schooling can be quite daunting. Nevertheless, armed with the right support networks, tools, and resources, the journey becomes more manageable, even if you're still geared up for challenges. So, where do you begin?

Before enrolling your child in school and initiating an Individualized Education Program (IEP), I strongly recommend conducting thorough research on the school you intend to choose.

28   Education

Additionally, paying a visit to the Washington State Office of Superintendent of Public Instruction, known as OSPI, could prove beneficial.

Visit: www.k12.wa.us

- Click on "Student Success."
- Explore "Special Education."
- Select "Early Childhood."

Here, you'll uncover insights into early developmental education available in your locality, along with contact details. It's worthwhile to drop them an email, inquiring about the necessary steps for enrolling your child in developmental preschool or kindergarten.

Moreover, take the time to acquaint yourself with Washington State's policies regarding restraints and isolation. Unfortunately, our state harbors some of the less favorable policies in this regard. Carefully scrutinize these policies, and in your child's IEP, make sure you express your preferences for handling meltdowns. I, personally, specified immediate contact and outlined precise actions to take during a meltdown. Further valuable information on IEPs can be found on the ARC website and OSPI, providing you with additional guidance as you embark on this journey.

What to Anticipate

The preschool phase is a thrilling period for children as they delve into new skills and cultivate relationships. Their reactions to various experiences contribute to their social, emotional, and academic growth during these years, which, in turn, plays a pivotal role in fostering brain development and building a solid foundation for lifelong well-being.

Yet, for parents navigating the realm of special education services, the commencement of preschool can be perplexing. Familiarizing yourself with the Individualized Education Program (IEP) and the 504 plan is imperative.

Special education services commence at age 3 and are orchestrated through school districts. Families collaborate with their special education team to determine the most suitable preschool arrangement for their child, weighing the options of a typical early childhood program versus a developmental program. This process is integral to crafting your child's personalized education plan, and you are a legally recognized member of the team.

In this guide, we will dissect crucial concepts and terminology, assisting you in making informed choices regarding preschool placement. We will also elucidate the distinction between developmental and standard early childhood programs.

Regarding Preschool

Inculcating a sense of belonging, membership, and participation holds great significance in the healthy development of childhood. The U.S. Department of Education and the U.S. Department of Health and Human Services jointly advocate the policy that "all young children with disabilities should have access to inclusive, high-quality early childhood programs, where they receive tailored and appropriate support to meet elevated expectations."

Their perspective on inclusive early childhood programs includes the following elements:

Embracing children with disabilities alongside their non-disabled peers.

Fostering high expectations and actively encouraging engagement in all learning and social activities, facilitated by personalized accommodations.

Employing evidence-based services and support to nurture diverse aspects of child development—cognitive, language, communication, physical, behavioral, and social-emotional—along with cultivating friendships and a sense of belonging.

This principle extends to all children with disabilities, ranging from those with milder challenges to those with more significant disabilities.

Research

Decades of research consistently underscore the superior outcomes stemming from high-quality, inclusive settings. Interestingly, studies examining social outcomes have failed to establish segregated settings as superior. In fact, non-inclusive environments have shown adverse effects on learning. On the contrary, inclusion proves advantageous, benefiting all children, irrespective of their disability status. Key factors in fostering inclusion include higher ratios of non-disabled children and substantial time spent in standard early childhood programs.

Restricted Environments

The Individuals with Disabilities Education Act (IDEA) serves as the federal framework for special education. While the term "inclusion" might not be explicitly used in IDEA, federal law demonstrates a preference for educating students with disabilities in general education classrooms, side by side with their non-disabled peers. IDEA underscores the concept of the least restrictive environment (LRE).

LRE encompasses both the learning environment and the provided services. If a child isn't placed in a standard early learning program, their IEP must offer a rationale. Preschool LRE can be realized across a range of settings, including public or private preschool programs, transitional or standard kindergarten, community-based childcare, or even within the child's home.

How is Placement Determined?

This pertains to the amount of time your child spends in the general education environment, alongside their non-disabled peers. Preschool programs can vary from fully inclusive to segregated. The IEP team, which includes you, collaboratively decides on the most fitting placement.

Alternative Placement Options

The Individuals with Disabilities Education Act (IDEA) mandates that school districts provide a range of alternative placement options. The least restrictive or most integrated placement is a standard early childhood program, where most support services are offered. In a regular program, at least half of the class consists of students without an Individualized Education Program (IEP). The available alternative placements encompass:

- Regular early childhood program with the majority of services provided off-site.
- Separate classroom or school.
- Home-based instruction.
- Residential facility.
- Location provided by another service provider.

According to IDEA, the presumed placement is the environment in which children would be educated if they didn't have disabilities. Children should only be removed from the regular education setting if the regular placement remains unsatisfactory despite the provision of supplementary aids, services, training, and technical assistance for administrators and teachers.

Addressing a Lack of Regular Early Childhood Programs

If your school district does not offer a standard early childhood program, your child still holds the right to the least restrictive environment. School districts are mandated to provide a free and appropriate public education in the least restrictive environment, even if they don't operate preschools for children without disabilities. This may involve delivering special education services in public or private standard early childhood programs, including Head Start or Early Childhood Education and Assistance Programs (ECEAP), or community-based childcare.

Insights into Washington State Practices

In comparison to other regions, Washington State stands as an outlier due to its tendency to segregate children with disabilities. According to the 2020 report to Congress on IDEA implementation, Washington ranked 49 out of 53 for inclusive preschool placements. The state displayed the fourth-highest rate for separate settings and the fourth-lowest rate for placement in a standard early childhood program with integrated supports. This trend persists into K-12 years, especially for children with intellectual disabilities. The report surveyed the 50 states, Puerto Rico, the District of Columbia (D.C.), and the Bureau of Indian Education. While efforts are underway to enhance and expand inclusion practices, implementation varies widely at the local level.

Your Entitlements

Your child possesses an equal right to education within the most integrated setting appropriate, bolstered by the necessary supports to ensure accessibility. In determining appropriateness, established practices and research play a pivotal role. The law assumes that the primary consideration for placement should be in a regular early childhood program, alongside non-disabled children, with supports seamlessly integrated.

Should the IEP team contemplate placing your child in a program where the majority or all students have disabilities, this deviates from an inclusive setting and may conflict with verified research. It's essential to seek a deeper understanding of why the IEP team deems this program suitable for your child, particularly concerning social development. The research strongly advocates for inclusion, and federal law presumes that the initial consideration for placement should be in a regular early childhood program, complemented by supports. If your school district lacks a standard early childhood program or available space within such a program, the IEP team can explore placement in a community program.

Things to keep in mind

- Inclusion is a right under federal anti-discrimination law and does not require earning.

- Children are not obliged to demonstrate their ability to thrive without supports. The least restrictive environment assumes that appropriate supports are in place.

- IEP teams must have research-backed and data-supported reasons to consider alternative placements over a regular early childhood program. A district's lack of a program or available space does not override a child's entitlement to the least restrictive environment.

Exploring Available Choices

Preschool options can vary significantly between different school districts and local communities. Let's delve into the array of possibilities you might encounter.

Developmental Preschools: Many Washington school districts employ the term "developmental preschools" to describe separate classes or schools tailored for preschoolers with disabilities. These classes are led by specialized education staff. Typically, they do not fulfill the criteria of a regular early childhood program, either because they exclusively enroll children with disabilities or have only a few non-disabled peers. However, some classes strike a balance with a 50-50 mix of children with and without disabilities. To meet the criteria of a regular early childhood program, at least half the class must consist of children without disabilities.

Regular Early Childhood Program: These programs cater to all children and encompass a minimum of 50% of students without disabilities. These programs are usually headed by general education staff, while specialized services are coordinated by special education staff. Co-teaching models are also prevalent. Such programs can be either school-based or community-based.

ECEAP (Early Childhood Education and Assistance Program): ECEAP focuses on holistic child well-being by providing comprehensive services, including family support. It aligns with the standards of a regular early childhood program and serves a similar percentage of students with disabilities as public K-12 schools. While all children qualifying for preschool special education services are eligible for ECEAP, securing a spot is not guaranteed due to limited space. The state is actively expanding ECEAP to meet demand. ECEAP programs are community-based and often collaborate with local school districts.

Head Start: Head Start initiatives aim to enhance the school readiness of infants, toddlers, and preschool-aged children from low-income families. Services are offered across various settings. This is a federal program, with a minimum requirement of 10% of Head Start slots allocated for students using special education services.

Community-Based Early Childhood Programs: These encompass public and private programs serving young children. Examples include ECEAP and Head Start, alongside alternatives like the Seattle Preschool Program and the Experimental Educational Unit at the Haring Center.

Mixed Programs: Occasionally, schools house regular early childhood programs that intertwine funding sources and include children from a mixture of programs.

Legal Aspects

Besides the IDEA, there are two additional federal anti-discrimination laws parents should acquaint themselves with. These laws collectively advocate for inclusion, remove barriers, and safeguard children with disabilities from discrimination.

Section 504

- Removes barriers and shields individuals with disabilities from discrimination.
- Prohibits organizations receiving federal funds from excluding or denying individuals with disabilities equal access to program benefits and services.
- Defines the rights of individuals with disabilities to participate in and access program benefits and services.
- Mandate school districts to provide a Free Appropriate Public Education (FAPE) to students with disabilities, regardless of the nature or severity of their disabilities.

The Individuals with Disabilities Education Act (IDEA)

- Funded through a grant, IDEA supports services for a specific group of students, in return for adherence to its regulations.
- Established in 1975 as the Education for All Handicapped Children Act, IDEA introduces:
- Child Find, requiring school districts to identify and evaluate students who may have disabilities.

- Parental rights to participate in IEP teams and decision-making.
- Individualized Education Programs (IEPs).
- Least Restrictive Environment (LRE).
- Procedural safeguards, laying the groundwork for collaboration between schools and families.

IDEA, is like Section 504, it mandates a Free Appropriate Public Education within the most suitable integrated environment.

Americans with Disabilities Act (ADA)

- Prohibits most instances of discrimination against individuals with disabilities.
- Title II: Bars state and local governments, including school districts, from discriminatory actions based on disability.
- Title III: Prevents disability-based discrimination in public accommodations, encompassing childcare providers and community-based preschools not affiliated with religious institutions.
- ADA doesn't generally apply to schools or programs operated by religious organizations, except for programs held in religious buildings but not religiously affiliated.

ADA guidance from the Washington State Department of Health underscores

- ADA necessitates child-care homes and centers to reasonably modify their policies and practices to integrate children with disabilities, unless this would fundamentally alter the program.

38 Education

- Centers must offer appropriate auxiliary aids and services to ensure effective communication with children with disabilities, provided this doesn't constitute an undue burden.
- Centers cannot exclude children with disabilities unless their presence poses a direct threat to others' health or safety or necessitates fundamental program alterations.

Reasonable modifications refer to changes that can be implemented without excessive difficulty or expense. Examples encompass policy adjustments, eliminating physical barriers, staff training, and supplying adaptive equipment. Auxiliary aids and services span a variety of devices or services aiding communication, such as sign language, interpreters, large print materials, and other communication equipment. Notably, hearing aids are excluded.

Developmental Preschool Explained

What is Developmental Preschool?

A developmental preschool, situated within your school district, offers educational services for children aged 3 to 4. These preschools can fall into two categories: inclusive classrooms that accommodate both children with learning disabilities and neurotypical children, or classrooms exclusively designed for children with special needs. In my view, striving for inclusion is ideal, where your child participates in an inclusive classroom with available services. This could entail having a paraeducator or behavioral therapist to provide support within the classroom. If you have the opportunity, consider volunteering at your child's school; this can be immensely enriching and beneficial, especially if your child requires your presence.

Understanding IEP and 504 Plans

Both IEP and 504 plans cater to children with special needs, although they differ in their offerings. You'll likely require an Individualized Education Plan (IEP), which stands for 'Individualized Education Plan.' While having both an IEP and a 504 plan is possible, everything encompassed in a 504 plan can be incorporated into your IEP. Given the inherent stress of managing one plan, it's advisable to focus on one that suits your child's needs best.

What is an IEP?

An Individualized Education Plan (IEP) is a personalized program designed to safeguard your child's educational journey, ensuring they receive the necessary support. This encompasses services, assistance, specialized instructions, and accommodations tailored to meet your child's learning and developmental requirements. An IEP must be reviewed at least once a year, but you can revisit and modify it as often as necessary. You're empowered to include anyone in the IEP process who you believe would offer valuable support—whether it's your spouse, family member, medical professionals, private therapists, advocates, or friends. Crafting an IEP is a collaborative effort; you don't have to navigate it alone. The IEP is supported by the "Individuals with Disabilities Education Act" (IDEA), as noted by the U.S. Department of Education.

Are all educators required to follow an IEP?

Learning coaches, paraeducators, and anyone directly involved in your child's education are generally expected to follow an Individualized Education Program (IEP) when working with students who have special educational needs. An IEP is a legally binding document that outlines educational goals, services, accommodations, and adjustments tailored to meet the specific needs of students with disabilities. These learning coaches, also known as educational aides, paraprofessionals, or instructional assistants, primarily provide support to students requiring extra guidance within the classroom, a group that includes individuals with unique needs.

The IEP serves as a roadmap for providing appropriate education and support to students facing disabilities. Within this framework, learning coaches play an essential role in implementing strategies and accommodations as outlined in the IEP. Working closely with teachers, special education experts, and other school staff, they ensure that the individualized needs of the student are addressed. This may involve offering one-on-one support, assisting with assignments, implementing behavioral interventions, or aiding in communication, depending on the specific requirements of the student and the goals set forth in the IEP.

For learning coaches, it's crucial to have a comprehensive understanding of the student's IEP and to collaborate closely with the broader educational team to maintain consistency in guidance and support. Adhering to the IEP promotes an inclusive and supportive learning environment that maximizes the student's potential for success.

U.S. Department of Education

"The IDEA governs how states and public agencies provide early intervention, special education, and related services to more than 7.5

Education 41

million (as of the 2020-21 school year) eligible infants, toddlers, children, and youth with disabilities."

"The law acknowledges that disability is a natural aspect of the human experience and does not diminish an individual's right to participate in society. Enhancing educational outcomes for children with disabilities is a fundamental aspect of our national commitment to ensuring equal opportunity, full participation, independent living, and economic self-sufficiency for individuals with disabilities."

What is a 504 Plan?

A 504 plan, like an IEP, caters to children who don't require special education but need accommodations due to disabilities. This plan addresses classroom needs, providing assistance and accommodations—such as specialized furniture—to overcome learning obstacles. The purpose is to eliminate barriers to learning. It's important to note that the 504 plan falls under Section 504 of the Rehabilitation Act and is guided by the Americans with Disabilities Act (ADA).

Difference between IEP and 504

The distinction between a 504 plan and an Individualized Education Program (IEP) lies in the specific educational accommodations and services they provide to students with varying needs. Both plans are designed to ensure that students with disabilities receive appropriate support and equal access to education, but they have key differences in terms of eligibility, scope, and the level of individualization offered.

504 Plan

A 504 plan like mentioned falls under Section 504 of the Rehabilitation Act of 1973, a federal law that prohibits discrimination against individuals with disabilities in programs and activities that receive federal funding. The main purpose of a 504 plan is to ensure that students with disabilities can participate fully and equally in the general education environment. This plan covers students with disabilities that substantially limit a major life activity, which can include learning, walking, seeing, hearing, and more. The disabilities covered under a 504 plan can be wide-ranging and include conditions like ADHD, diabetes, anxiety, and allergies, among others.

Key Features of a 504 Plan

1. Eligibility Criteria: To be eligible for a 504 plan, a student must have a disability that substantially limits a major life activity, as determined through a formal evaluation process.
2. Accommodations: 504 plans primarily provide assistance such as extended time on tests, preferential seating, modified assignments, assistive technology, and accessibility adjustments.
3. General Education: Students with 504 plans are generally educated in the mainstream or general education setting, with accommodations tailored to their specific needs.

IEP (Individualized Education Program)

An IEP, on the other hand, is mandated by the Individuals with Disabilities Education Act (IDEA), a federal law that ensures a free and appropriate public education (FAPE) to students with disabilities. The IEP is a comprehensive, legally binding document that outlines an individualized plan for the education of students with more significant disabilities that require specialized instruction and services.

Key Features of an IEP

- Eligibility Criteria: To qualify for an IEP, a student must have a disability that adversely affects educational performance and requires specialized instruction.
- Individualized Goals: The IEP includes personalized academic, developmental, and functional goals that are specific to the student's needs.
- Services: In addition to accommodations, an IEP may include specialized services such as speech therapy, occupational therapy, physical therapy, counseling, and more.
- Specialized Education: Students with IEPs often receive education in a specialized classroom or setting, which may include resource rooms, self-contained classrooms, or special education schools, depending on the severity of their needs.
- Progress Monitoring: The IEP outlines how the student's progress will be measured and evaluated, with periodic reviews to determine the effectiveness of the plan.

In summary, while both 504 plans and IEPs aim to provide support to students with disabilities, the key distinction lies in the level of disability and the extent of services required. 504 plans are generally for students who require accommodations to access the general education curriculum, whereas IEPs are designed for students with more significant disabilities that necessitate specialized instruction and services beyond what can be provided in a mainstream classroom.

What is OSPI and why are they important?

The Office of Superintendent of Public Instruction (OSPI) is the primary agency responsible for overseeing K-12 education in the state of Washington. OSPI's main role is to provide leadership, guidance, and support to school districts, educators, and students to ensure a high-quality education for all students in the state. This includes students with disabilities, including those with autism.

OSPI's responsibilities include

Setting Educational Standards: OSPI establishes academic standards and learning goals for students in Washington state. These standards help guide curriculum development and ensure that students receive a well-rounded education.

Providing Resources: OSPI offers a variety of resources, instructional materials, and guidelines for educators to support effective teaching and learning.

Supporting Special Education: OSPI plays a key role in overseeing special education programs and services. They provide guidance to school districts on how to implement special education laws and regulations, including those related to students with autism.

Ensuring Compliance: OSPI ensures that school districts are in compliance with federal and state laws regarding special education, including the Individuals with Disabilities Education Act (IDEA). This includes ensuring that students with disabilities receive appropriate services, accommodations, and individualized education plans (IEPs).

Professional Development: OSPI offers professional development opportunities for educators to enhance their skills and knowledge in working with students with disabilities, including autism.

Monitoring and Accountability: OSPI monitors the progress of students with disabilities and holds school districts accountable for providing equitable education opportunities. They also collect and report data on student outcomes.

How OSPI can protect your child with autism

- Access to Services: OSPI ensures that students with autism have access to appropriate special education services and supports in accordance with their individual needs and rights under federal and state laws.

- Inclusive Education: OSPI promotes the inclusion of students with autism in general education settings whenever possible, ensuring that they have access to the same academic curriculum and extracurricular activities as their peers.

- Individualized Education Plans (IEPs): OSPI oversees the development and implementation of IEPs, which are tailored education plans for students with disabilities, including autism. These plans outline the specific accommodations, goals, and services that your child will receive to support their learning.

Parent and Family Rights: OSPI ensures that parents of children with autism are aware of their rights and can actively participate in the education and decision-making process for their child's education.

If you have concerns or questions about your child's education, including their rights as a student with autism, you can reach out to OSPI for guidance. Additionally, connecting with your child's school's special education department and collaborating with teachers and school staff can help ensure that your child's needs are being met effectively.

Charter schools, Public schools, Private schools, and Cooperative schools

Charter Schools

Charter schools are publicly funded institutions that operate independently under a charter granted by a governing body, such as a school district or a state agency. They often have more flexibility in their curriculum and teaching methods compared to traditional public schools. Charter schools vary widely in how they address the needs of children with autism. Some charter schools specialize in providing tailored support for children with autism, using evidence-based practices and specialized programs. However, the level of support and resources can vary greatly depending on the specific charter school.

Public Schools

Public schools are government-funded institutions that provide education to students in the community. They are legally obligated to provide a free and appropriate public education (FAPE) to children with disabilities, including autism, under the Individuals with Disabilities Education Act (IDEA). Public schools offer a range of special education services and accommodations for students with autism, including Individualized Education Programs (IEPs) and access to various support services such as speech therapy, occupational therapy, and behavioral interventions.

Private Schools

Private schools are funded by tuition, donations, and often operate independently from government regulations. While private schools may not be required to provide special education services to the same extent as public schools, some do offer specialized programs for children with autism. These programs can vary widely in terms of quality, staff expertise, and resources. Parents who choose private schools for their child with autism should carefully research the school's approach to special education and the support they offer.

Cooperative Schools

Cooperative schools, also known as co-op schools, are educational institutions where parents are actively involved in the operation and management of the school. These schools can be public or private and may have a unique approach to education. When it comes to children with autism, the level of support in cooperative schools can vary depending on the school's resources and the collective decisions made by parents. Some cooperative schools may prioritize inclusive education and work to create a supportive environment for children with autism, while others may have limited resources for specialized services.

In summary, the differences between charter schools, public schools, private schools, and cooperative schools in their approach to serving children with autism largely depend on their funding sources, regulations, and individual philosophies. It's important for parents of children with autism to carefully research and consider each school's offerings, staff expertise, and track record in providing effective support and education for children with autism before making a decision.

Questions to ask

Registering a child with autism into a school requires careful consideration to ensure that the school can provide the necessary support and education tailored to their needs. Here are some important questions that parents should ask before enrolling their child with autism into any school:

- How experienced is the staff in working with children with autism?
  - Inquire about the qualifications, training, and experience of teachers, special education staff, therapists, and other professionals who will be working with your child.

- What is the school's approach to special education and inclusion?
  - Understand how the school supports inclusive education, and if they have experience integrating children with autism into mainstream classrooms.

- What specialized services are available?
  - Ask about the availability of speech therapy, occupational therapy, behavioral therapy, and any other specialized services your child might need.

- Do they offer Individualized Education Programs (IEPs) or 504 plans?
    - Learn how the school develops and implements individualized plans to address your child's unique needs.
- How do they handle behavioral challenges?
    - Inquire about the school's behavioral interventions and strategies for managing challenging behaviors.

- What communication methods are used?
    - Understand how the school communicates with parents about their child's progress, challenges, and achievements.

- Are there sensory-friendly environments?
    - Ask about the availability of sensory-friendly spaces and accommodations to create a comfortable learning environment for children with autism.

- What is the student-to-staff ratio?
    - Understand the class sizes and the ratio of students to teachers or aides, as a lower ratio can often provide more individualized attention.

- How do they handle transitions and changes in routine?
    - Inquire about the school's approach to helping children with autism navigate transitions and changes, which can often be challenging.

- Are there opportunities for social interaction and peer relationships?
    - Ask about social skills programs and opportunities for your child to interact with peers in structured and unstructured settings.

- How does the school address sensory needs?
    - Understand how the school accommodates sensory sensitivities and provides sensory breaks if needed.

- What professional development is provided to staff?
    - Learn about ongoing training and professional development opportunities for staff to stay updated on best practices for working with children with autism.

- Can you visit and observe classes?
    - Request to visit the school and observe classrooms to get a sense of the environment and how children with autism are supported.

- What is the school's philosophy on inclusion and diversity?
    - Understand the school's commitment to fostering an inclusive and diverse environment.

- Can you connect with other parents of children with autism in the school?

- Connect with other parents to get their perspective on their child's experience at the school.

Remember that each child with autism is unique, so tailor these questions to your child's specific needs and priorities. It's crucial to gather as much information as possible to make an informed decision that supports your child's growth and development.

IEP and 504 example

Below is a basic template for both an Individualized Education Program (IEP) and a 504 Plan, but please keep in mind that these templates should serve as starting points and need to be customized to your child's specific needs, goals, and the legal requirements of your state. It's highly recommended to work with your child's school and a qualified special education professional to develop these plans properly.

Here's a simple sample template for each:

(Note: This is just a brief example)

Individualized Education Program (IEP) for: [Child's Name]

Date: [Date]

Student Information:

- **Name:** [Child's Name]
- **Date of Birth:** [Date of Birth]
- **School:** [School Name]
- **Grade:** [Grade]

Present Levels of Performance:

[Describe your child's current academic, functional, and social abilities, as well as any challenges they face.]

Goals and Objectives:

[Specify measurable goals and objectives for your child's academic, functional, and social development.]

Special Education and Related Services:

- **Service(s):** [List the specific services, therapies, and supports your child will receive.]
- **Frequency and Duration:** [Specify how often and for how long each service will be provided.]

Accommodations and Modifications:

[Outline the accommodations and modifications your child will receive to access the curriculum and participate in school activities.]

Participation in General Education:

[Explain how your child will be included in general education settings and activities.]

Transition Services (if applicable):

[Detail any transition services or plans for post-secondary education, vocational training, employment, or independent living.]

Parent and Student Participation:

[Indicate the participation of parents and the student in the IEP development and review process.]

Signatures:

- Parent/Guardian Signature: _____ Date: _____

- Student Signature (if applicable): ____ Date: _____
- School Representative (Principal): ____ Date: _____
- School Representative (General Ed Teacher): ____ Date: _____
- School Representative (SPED teacher): ___ Date: _____
- School Representative (SLP): _____ Date: _____
- School Representative (OT): _____ Date: _____

(Include any extra teachers, aides, therapists, or psychologists who will be part of your child's school team.)

This IEP will be reviewed and updated on: [Review Date].

504 Plan Template

Section 504 Plan for: [Child's Name]

Date: [Date]

Student Information:

- **Name:** [Child's Name]
- **Date of Birth:** [Date of Birth]
- **School:** [School Name]
- **Grade:** [Grade]

Diagnosis and Eligibility:

[Explain the child's diagnosis of autism and how it substantially limits a major life activity.]

Accommodations and Supports:

[Detail the accommodations, modifications, and supports that will be provided to meet your child's needs.]

Parent and School Responsibilities:

- **Parent/Guardian Responsibilities:** [List any responsibilities or tasks for parents/guardians.]
- **School Responsibilities:** [List any responsibilities or tasks for school staff.]

Review and Updates:

[Specify how often the 504 Plan will be reviewed and updated.]

Signatures:

- Parent/Guardian Signature: _____ Date: _____
- School Representative: _____ Date: _____

(Include any extra teachers, aides, therapists, or psychologists who will be part of your child's school team.)

This 504 Plan will be reviewed and updated on: [Review Date].

Remember that these templates are simplified and should be adapted to your child's unique needs, goals, and the legal requirements of your state. It's important to collaborate with your child's school and a qualified special education professional to ensure that the plans are comprehensive and appropriate.

Advocates

Finding an autism advocate for Individualized Education Plans (IEPs) in Washington State can greatly benefit your child's educational experience. An IEP is a legal document outlining the

Education 55

special education services a child with a disability will receive in a public school. An advocate can help ensure that your child's rights are upheld and that they receive the appropriate services and support.

Steps to find an autism advocate for IEPs in Washington State:

- Research Advocacy Organizations: Look for advocacy organizations in Washington State that specialize in autism and special education. These organizations often have resources, information, and may offer advocacy services or referrals.

- Online Search: Search online for autism advocates or special education advocates in Washington State. You can use search engines, social media platforms, and professional networking sites to find advocates with experience in IEPs.

- Local Autism Support Groups: Join local autism support groups or parent networks in your area. These groups can provide recommendations and referrals for trusted advocates who have helped other families navigate the IEP process.

- Contact School Districts: Some school districts have special education departments that can provide information about available advocates. They might have a list of recommended advocates or organizations to contact.

- Professional Directories: Check professional directories of advocates or attorneys who specialize in special education and autism advocacy. These directories often list the advocate's credentials, experience, and contact information.

What to consider

- Experience: Look for advocates who have experience working with children on the autism spectrum and have a solid understanding of special education laws and the IEP process.

- Credentials: Some advocates may hold certifications in special education advocacy or have legal backgrounds. These credentials can add to their expertise.
- References: Ask for references from other parents who have used their services. A reputable advocate should be able to provide references that can vouch for their effectiveness.
- Communication Skills: A good advocate should be an effective communicator who can clearly explain complex concepts, collaborate with school personnel, and represent your child's needs.
- Empathy and Dedication: Look for an advocate who is empathetic, understanding, and genuinely dedicated to advocating for your child's best interests.
- Fee Structure: Advocates typically charge for their services. Fees can vary widely based on the advocate's experience, location, and the complexity of the case.
- Initial Consultation: Many advocates offer a free initial consultation. During this meeting, you can discuss your concerns, learn about their approach, and decide if they are a good fit for your needs.
- Payment Options: Some advocates may offer sliding-scale fees based on income or payment plans to make their services more accessible.
- Free Advocacy Services: In Washington State, there are often nonprofit organizations or state-funded programs that offer free or low-cost advocacy services to families who may not be able to afford a private advocate. These services can vary by region.

Remember that laws and resources can change over time, so it's a good idea to do some recent research to find the most up-to-date information regarding autism advocates for IEPs in Washington State.

Finding a Specialist

Finding Doctors Specializing in Autism

Remember, it's crucial to request a written summary of the discussions and outcomes from each evaluation and meeting with every doctor and professional. Keeping a copy of these documents in your designated binder will help you maintain a comprehensive record of your child's progress and medical history.

When searching for a pediatrician who specializes in autism, consider the following steps:

Research: Look for pediatricians in your area who have experience or a special interest in autism spectrum disorder (ASD). You can use online directories, medical association websites, and autism advocacy groups to find potential doctors.

Recommendations: Reach out to local autism support groups, parent networks, or other families with children on the spectrum. They might have valuable recommendations based on their own experiences.

Check Credentials: Verify the doctor's credentials and qualifications. Look for board certification in pediatrics and any additional training or certifications related to autism or developmental disorders.

Schedule Consultations: Once you've identified potential doctors, schedule consultations to meet with them and discuss their approach to autism diagnosis, treatment, and ongoing care.

Questions to Ask Before Selecting a Doctor for Your Child with Autism

During your consultations, ask the following questions to determine if the pediatrician is the right fit for your child:

- What is your experience with diagnosing and treating autism?
- How do you approach autism diagnosis and assessment?
- What therapies and interventions do you recommend for children with autism?
- How do you collaborate with other specialists involved in my child's care?
- Can you provide referrals to other professionals, such as speech therapists or behavior therapists?
- How do you involve families in the treatment process?
- What is your philosophy regarding medication management for autism-related challenges?
- How often will we have follow-up appointments?
- Can you provide guidance on managing sensory sensitivities and behavioral challenges?
- How do you support transitions, such as from pediatric care to adult care?

Specialists for Children with Autism

Neurologist: Neurologists can help assess neurological aspects of autism and provide guidance on managing seizures or other neurological issues that some individuals with autism might experience.

Nutritionist: A nutritionist can provide guidance on managing dietary concerns and sensitivities that might be common in individuals with autism. They can help ensure a balanced diet and address any nutritional deficiencies.

Gastroenterologist: Gastrointestinal issues are often reported in individuals with autism. A gastroenterologist can help diagnose and manage digestive problems, which may impact overall well-being and behavior.

Naturopath: Some families explore alternative therapies for autism. A naturopath can offer holistic approaches to support health and well-being alongside conventional treatments.

Dentist: Dental care can be challenging for individuals with autism due to sensory sensitivities and communication difficulties. A dentist experienced in treating patients with special needs can provide appropriate care.

Optometrist: Visual processing challenges are common in autism. An optometrist can assess visual function and provide recommendations for vision therapy or specialized eyewear if needed.

Otolaryngologist: Individuals with autism may experience difficulties in communication, including speech and language delays. Otolaryngologists specialize in conditions related to the ear, nose, and throat, which are essential for speech development and hearing. Some individuals with autism might face challenges in hearing or speech due to anatomical or sensory factors. Otolaryngologists can help assess and address any hearing or speech-related issues, ensuring that individuals with autism have the necessary support to communicate effectively.

Sleep Apnea Specialist: Sleep disturbances are common among individuals with autism. Sleep problems, including sleep apnea, can significantly impact overall well-being, behavior, and cognitive functioning. Sleep apnea specialists are equipped to diagnose and treat sleep-related disorders. In the context of autism, addressing sleep issues is crucial as it can have a positive impact on the individual's daily life, mood regulation, and cognitive functioning.

Coordinating the efforts of these specialists, in conjunction with your child's pediatrician, can establish a holistic care strategy that's finely tuned to address your child's distinct requirements and hurdles. Emphasize transparent communication and a collaborative approach to attain optimal results for your child. Additionally, it's important to remember that you have the right to decline a doctor or professional if you feel it's not the right fit. You're the expert in your child's needs, and your aim is to construct the ideal team that best suits your family's requirements.

Outings

We all aspire to create lasting memories with our children and engage in various outings together. Nevertheless, when parenting a child on the autism spectrum, this endeavor can become challenging. Many establishments lack the necessary provisions for children with special needs. This often places the responsibility on us, the parents, and caregivers, to advocate for more inclusive environments for our children. While there are a handful of places in Washington that do offer accommodations for those on the spectrum, these are often limited to specific days or hours. Some establishments might provide only basic items like headphones or fidget toys, which can be a source of frustration. Despite these obstacles, I am dedicated to offering guidance on alternative approaches that ensure your child can enjoy experiences to the fullest extent possible.

Places

Seattle Children's Museum:

Location: 305 Harrison St, Seattle, WA

The museum offers sensory-friendly hours on certain dates, providing a quieter and less crowded environment for children with sensory sensitivities to explore interactive exhibits.

Pacific Science Center:

Location: 200 2nd Ave N, Seattle, WA

The Discovery Zone has sensory-friendly hours with reduced stimuli, allowing children to engage in hands-on science activities and exploration in a more comfortable environment.

Woodland Park Zoo:

Location: 5500 Phinney Ave N, Seattle, WA

Woodland Park Zoo hosts Sensory Saturdays, providing a quieter and more relaxed setting for families to enjoy the zoo. They offer sensory maps and tools to enhance the experience. There is no charge for your child's aid.

Imagine Children's Museum:

Location: 1502 Wall St, Everett, WA

The museum periodically offers "Play for All" hours, providing a sensory-friendly environment for children to play and learn with adjusted lighting and reduced noise.

Seattle Aquarium:

Location: 1483 Alaskan Way, Seattle, WA

The aquarium hosts Autism Early Open events with reduced sensory stimuli, allowing families to explore marine exhibits in a calm and inclusive atmosphere.

Point Defiance Zoo:

Location: 5400 N Pearl St, Tacoma, WA

The zoo offers sensory inclusive bags, has a sensory garden for little explorers and are known for increasing the understanding of inclusion and acceptance.

KidsQuest Children's Museum:

Location: 1116 108th Ave NE, Bellevue, WA

KidsQuest offers sensory-friendly playtimes for children with special needs, featuring modified lighting and a supportive environment for exploration and learning.

Seattle Children's Theatre:

Location: 201 Thomas St, Seattle, WA

The theater occasionally presents sensory-friendly performances of their shows, accommodating sensory sensitivities with adjusted sound and lighting.

Children's PlayGarden:

Location: 1745 24th Ave S, Seattle, WA

Children's PlayGarden is a unique outdoor play space designed for children of all abilities, including those with special needs. The garden promotes inclusive play and learning in a natural setting.

Hands On Children's Museum:

Location: 414 Jefferson St NE, Olympia, WA

The museum has sensory-friendly hours that provide an inclusive space for children to engage in interactive exhibits at their own pace.

Greentrike Children's Museum of Tacoma:

Location: 1501 Pacific Avenue, Tacoma, WA

This museum provide low sensory hours that are dedicated to providing a calm environment with reduced noise and light for families with sensory sensitivities.

Make sure to check the official websites or contact these places directly for the most up-to-date information regarding their sensory-friendly offerings, timings, and accommodations for children with special needs.

Creating your safe group

Creating a secure and supportive playgroup has been a significant step for my son's well-being. Regrettably, my encounters with online autism parent groups weren't as positive as I had hoped. Instead of finding the help and understanding I sought, I encountered judgment from other parents. However, when my son began attending the early childhood center, I took the opportunity to connect with parents during drop-offs and pick-ups, and also engaged with his teacher to identify his strongest connections.

Building upon these connections, I reached out to parents who seemed like a good fit for a playgroup involving our children. One of the common concerns among parents like us revolves around whether our children will have friends who genuinely comprehend and harmonize with them. Through the establishment of this playgroup, we've managed to address this concern successfully.

When organizing a playgroup, there are several considerations. Firstly, gauge your compatibility with the other parents. Do you feel at ease with them? Is this a circle in which you can be genuinely comfortable? Aligning viewpoints on child-rearing philosophies is vital, and even if differences arise, mutual respect should prevail. Compatibility extends to the children as well; do they get along well? It's critical that they get along well when they interact.

Furthermore, active involvement from all parents is vital. Sharing the responsibilities associated with the playgroup prevents you from shouldering everything alone, which can quickly become overwhelming. By distributing tasks, the burden becomes lighter for everyone involved, making the entire experience more enjoyable and sustainable.

Planning your playgroup

Creating a playgroup for a child with autism requires careful planning and consideration to ensure a positive and supportive environment. Here are some questions to ask, concerns to address, and things to want and expect when putting together a playgroup for your child with autism:

Questions to Ask

- What are the ages and developmental levels of the other children in the playgroup? It's important to match your child with peers who are close in age and developmental stage.

- What is the size of the playgroup? A smaller group may be less overwhelming and easier for your child to navigate.

- What are the interests and preferences of the other children? Finding common interests can help facilitate meaningful interactions.

- What is the planned structure and schedule of the playgroup? Knowing the routine can help your child anticipate activities and transitions.

- What qualifications or experience do the facilitators or organizers have with children with autism? It's beneficial to have individuals who understand autism and its nuances.

- What sensory considerations have been made? Ensure that the environment and activities are sensory-friendly and avoid triggers for sensory sensitivities.

- Are there any communication strategies in place? Ask how the playgroup will accommodate different communication styles, including nonverbal communication.

- What behavioral support strategies will be used, if needed? Inquire about how challenging behaviors will be managed and whether positive behavior support techniques will be employed.

- Is the playgroup inclusive and welcoming? Make sure that the playgroup environment is open to diversity and fosters a sense of belonging for all participants.

Concerns to Address

Sensory Sensitivities: Many children with autism have sensory sensitivities. Consider the noise levels, lighting, and textures in the play environment.

Social Interaction Challenges: Some children with autism struggle with social skills. Ensure that the playgroup encourages and supports social interactions in a patient and understanding manner.

Communication Differences: Be mindful of varying communication styles and provide opportunities for both verbal and nonverbal communication.

Safe space: Overstimulation is very common with children with autism, having a close confined space like a designated quiet room, a corner with soft cushions, or tent with dim lighting can be essential.

Transitions and Routine Changes: Sudden changes in routine can be difficult for children with autism. Discuss how transitions will be managed and whether there will be a consistent schedule.

Safety Measures: Address any safety concerns related to the play space, equipment, and potential wandering behavior.

Things to Want and Expect

Inclusivity and Acceptance: You should expect that the playgroup fosters an inclusive environment where your child is accepted for who they are.

Structured Activities: The playgroup should offer structured activities that cater to your child's interests and developmental level.

Understanding of Autism: Facilitators and organizers should have a basic understanding of autism and be willing to learn about your child's individual needs.

Clear Communication: Expect open and clear communication about the playgroup's activities, schedule, and any changes.

Positive Behavior Support: The playgroup should implement positive behavior support techniques that focus on reinforcing desired behaviors.

Flexibility: While structure is important, some flexibility should be allowed to accommodate the diverse needs of children with autism.

Parent Involvement: You should be welcomed and encouraged to participate in the playgroup, providing insights and support for your child's interactions.

Progress Tracking: Ideally, the playgroup should track your child's progress in social interactions, communication, and other relevant areas.

Remember, every child with autism is unique, so it's important to tailor the playgroup experience to your child's individual strengths and challenges. Collaboration with facilitators, other parents, and professionals can lead to a positive playgroup experience for your child.

Accommodations and Inclusivity

If you encounter an organization that doesn't provide accommodations or support for children with autism, here's what you can do and ask:

Communicate Your Concerns

Reach out to the organization's management or relevant staff members and express your concerns about the lack of accommodations for children with autism. Be respectful but clear about the needs and challenges faced by individuals with autism.

Inquire About Plans

Ask whether the organization has any plans to include accommodations for children with autism in the future. This can give your insight into their commitment to inclusivity.

Share Information

Provide educational resources or information about the benefits of accommodations for children with autism. This could help the organization understand the importance of making these changes.

Ask for Reasoning

Inquire about the reasons behind the current lack of accommodations. Understanding their perspective can help you address their concerns and find potential solutions.

Request Collaboration

Suggest collaborating with the organization to explore possible accommodations. Offer to share information, resources, or even connect them with experts who can help design autism-friendly environments.

Propose Solutions:

Offer specific suggestions for accommodations that could be implemented, such as early entrance, low lights, sensory-friendly spaces, or visual supports. Highlight how these changes can benefit both the children with autism and the organization.

Advocate for Change:

If the organization is unresponsive, consider advocating for change by involving other parents, community members, or advocacy groups that focus on autism awareness and inclusion.

Seek External Support:

If necessary, contact local autism support organizations or advocacy groups for advice and assistance. They might have experience in working with similar situations and can offer guidance.

Consider Alternatives:

If the organization remains unwilling to make accommodations, explore alternative options for your child's activities or services. Look for places that prioritize inclusivity and provide a supportive environment for children with autism.

Stay Persistent:

Advocating for change can take time. Stay persistent and keep the lines of communication open. Your efforts may lead to positive changes over time.

Remember, your advocacy efforts can have a positive impact not only on your child but also on the larger community by promoting inclusivity and awareness about the needs of individuals with autism.

Here's a template letter that you can use as a starting point to address organizations about being more inclusive for children with autism:

[Your Name]

[City, State, ZIP]

[Email Address]

[Phone Number]

[Date]

[Organization's Name]

[Organization's Address]

[City, State, ZIP]

Dear [Recipient's Name],

I hope this letter finds you well. My name is [Your Name], and I am writing to you as a concerned parent and advocate for children with autism.

I recently became aware of your [event/program/organization] and was excited about the opportunities it offers to children. However, I noticed that there might be some areas where inclusivity for children with autism could be enhanced.

I believe that creating an inclusive environment is not only beneficial for children with autism but for the entire community as well. By making a few thoughtful accommodations, you have the opportunity to provide a more welcoming and enriching experience for all children, regardless of their abilities. Here are some reasons why prioritizing inclusivity is important:

- Promoting Diversity: An inclusive environment helps foster a diverse and understanding community, where everyone feels valued and respected for their uniqueness.
- Ensuring Equal Opportunities: Accommodations can provide children with autism the same opportunities to participate, learn, and enjoy the experience as their peers.
- Raising Awareness: By creating an inclusive space, you raise awareness about the needs and challenges faced by individuals with autism, promoting understanding and acceptance.
- Building Stronger Relationships: Encouraging interactions between children with and without autism can lead to stronger friendships, empathy, and social skills development for all.
- Enhancing Community Reputation: Being known as an organization that prioritizes inclusivity can positively impact your reputation and attract families who seek welcoming and supportive environments.

I kindly ask if you would consider implementing some autism-friendly accommodations such as:

- Early entrance or quieter check-in options to reduce sensory overload.

- Providing sensory-friendly spaces for children who might need a quiet space to calm down.

- Incorporating visual supports, such as schedules and instructions, to help children understand and follow the activities.

- Offering training to staff members about interacting with children with autism and recognizing their unique strengths and challenges.

I am more than willing to offer my support and resources to assist in implementing these accommodations. I believe that together, we can make [event/program/organization] an even more inclusive and enriching experience for all children involved.

Thank you for taking the time to consider my suggestions. I am looking forward to hearing your thoughts and discussing how we can collaborate to create a more inclusive environment. Please feel free to reach out to me at [your email address] or [your phone number].

Warm regards,

[Your Name]

Remember to personalize the template with specific details about the organization and your concerns. Providing examples and showing your willingness to collaborate can increase the likelihood of a positive response.

Day trips, road trips and flying what to pack, expect and prepare.

Below are lists of items to consider packing for various types of outings:

Please note that every child's needs are unique, these items may be applicable to your child. Nonetheless, this list is intended to offer a starting point to assist you.

Daytime Outings

Communication Tools:

- Communication device or AAC app: These tools enable the child to express their needs, preferences, and feelings effectively, even in unfamiliar environments.
- PEC cards: PEC cards provide a visual way for the child to communicate their desires or needs when interacting with others.

Comfort Items:

- Favorite comfort toy or stuffed animal.
- Sensory items like fidget toys, stress balls, or a weighted blanket.

Snacks and Drinks: (Avoid any snacks/drinks that can cause overstimulation such as sugars and dyes)

- Snacks that your child enjoys and can easily eat.
- Drinks in spill-proof containers.

First Aid Kit:

- Basic first aid supplies including band-aids, antiseptic wipes, and any necessary medications.

Change of Clothes:

- Extra set of clothes in case of spills or accidents.

Sensory Comfort:

- Noise-canceling headphones or earplugs for noisy environments.
- Sunglasses or a visor to help with bright lights.
- Sensory toys such as fidgets or a chewy
- Weighted blanket or stuffy
-

Road Trips

In addition to the items above, consider packing:

Communication Tools:

- AAC devices: Long road trips may require ongoing communication, and AAC devices can help the child engage with others and stay entertained.
- PEC cards: Using PEC cards can help the child communicate wants and needs while on the road.

Entertainment:

- Tablets, electronic devices, or favorite toys for entertainment during the journey.

Comfort on the Go:

- Travel-sized sensory items like a mini weighted lap pad or travel-sized fidget toys.

Music and Audio:

- Favorite music or calming audio tracks on a device.

Window Shades:

- Car window shades to block out excess sunlight. This can be a major sensitivity trigger for some kids.

Travel Potty (if applicable):

- Portable potty or toilet training supplies if your child is potty training. Some children on the spectrum can have severe anxiety in public restrooms.

Flying

In addition to the items mentioned earlier, consider packing:

Communication Tools:
- AAC devices: In the busy and potentially overwhelming environment of an airport and airplane, AAC devices provide a consistent means of communication for the child.
- PEC cards: PEC cards can assist the child in communicating with flight attendants, fellow passengers, and caregivers throughout the journey.

Documentation:
- Copies of any necessary medical or identification documents.

In-Flight Entertainment:
- Earphones or headphones for in-flight entertainment systems.
- Portable entertainment devices with favorite movies or games.

Chewable Snacks:
- Snacks that can help alleviate ear discomfort during takeoff and landing.

Comfort in a Confined Space:

- Small travel pillow for head or neck support.

Medications:

- Carry any necessary medications in their original packaging.

Note: If you have check-in luggage with medical supplies there should be no charge

Plan for Sensory Needs:

- Noise-canceling headphones or earplugs to manage sensory overload in the airplane cabin.

Remember that each child is unique, so customize the lists based on your child's specific needs and preferences. It's also a good idea to consult with their healthcare provider before traveling to ensure you have all necessary medications and medical information on hand.

TSA Cares and Arc Wings Program

TSA Cares and the Arc Wings program offer essential aid to individuals with disabilities, including those on the autism spectrum.

TSA Cares:

TSA Cares is a program provided by the Transportation Security Administration (TSA), dedicated to ensuring a smooth and comfortable airport security screening process for travelers with disabilities and medical conditions. Travelers can reach out to TSA Cares at least 72 hours before their flight to arrange assistance and discuss their unique needs.

TSA Cares include:

Specialized Support: Passengers with disabilities can request assistance from TSA personnel who are trained to deliver specialized aid.

Informing About Needs: Travelers can inform TSA Cares agents about any medical conditions, disabilities, or specific requirements to facilitate a tailored screening experience.

Guidance and Information: TSA Cares offers valuable insights into the screening procedure, security regulations, and guidelines for carrying medical equipment and supplies.

Arc Wings Program:

The Arc Wings program is a resource extended by The Arc, a prominent organization advocating for individuals with intellectual and developmental disabilities. This program offers valuable support and guidance to travelers with disabilities, ensuring they embark on positive travel journeys.

Arc Wings program offers

Preparation Insights: The program presents comprehensive travel preparation information, including advice on documentation, packing, and effective communication with airline staff.

Travel Toolkits: The Arc provides travel toolkits that encompass essential resources for various travel types, such as air travel, cruises, and road trips.

Advocacy and Backing: Arc Wings empowers travelers to understand their rights, advocate for their requirements, and navigate potential challenges during their travel experience.

82 Flying

Travel Narratives: The program showcases personal travel accounts from individuals with disabilities, inspiring and reassuring others about the possibility of enjoyable travel.

Here is the contact information for both TSA Cares and The Arc Wings program:

TSA Cares:

Website: TSA Cares:

https://www.tsa.gov/travel/passenger-support/tsa-cares

Phone: 1-855-787-2227

Email: TSA-ContactCenter@tsa.dhs.gov

The Arc Wings Program:

Website: The Arc Wings Program: https://thearc.org/travel/

Phone: 1-800-433-5255

Email: info@thearc.org

Feel free to visit their websites or use the provided contact details to obtain more information and assistance related to travel support for individuals with disabilities, including those on the autism spectrum.

Social Stories

Social stories are amazing tools that provide structure, predictability, and understanding for children on the autism spectrum. This is particularly crucial when traveling, as new environments, routines, and sensory experiences can be overwhelming and anxiety-inducing for these children. Social stories offer several benefits:

- Predictability: Children with autism often thrive on routine and predictability. Social stories outline the sequence of events during a trip, helping the child anticipate what will happen next, reducing uncertainty and anxiety.
- Visual Support: Social stories use visual cues, such as pictures and simple language, making them easier for children with autism to comprehend. Visual supports aid understanding by providing concrete representations of abstract concepts.
- Managing Sensory Overload: Travel often exposes children to unfamiliar sensory experiences. Social stories can prepare children for potential sensory challenges, helping them cope and remain calmer during overwhelming moments.
- Communication Enhancement: Social stories can improve communication skills by introducing vocabulary and phrases related to travel. This can aid the child in expressing their needs, feelings, and concerns.
- Behavioral Expectations: Social stories clarify expected behaviors in various situations, promoting appropriate conduct during travel. This helps reduce confusion and meltdowns by setting clear expectations.
- Empowerment and Independence: When children know what to expect, they feel more in control of their environment. Social stories empower them to participate more actively in their travel experience.

Obtaining Social Stories

Online Resources: Numerous websites offer free or purchasable social stories tailored to various travel scenarios. Websites like Teachers Pay Teachers, Autism Speaks, and Boardmaker often provide such resources. After you become comfortable with social stories, creating your own is a straightforward process using Microsoft Word.

Specialized Apps: Some apps are designed to create and access social stories. These apps allow you to customize stories to fit your child's specific needs and preferences.

Creating Social Stories

- Focus on the Target Situation: Identify the specific travel situations that might be challenging for your child, such as airport security, boarding the plane, or staying in a hotel.
- Use Clear and Simple Language: Write sentences in a concise and straightforward manner. Use visuals to complement the text.
- Visuals: Include images or pictures that represent each step of the situation. These visuals help the child better understand the process.
- Positive Tone: Frame the story positively, highlighting the fun aspects of the trip and the child's capabilities.
- Repetition and Reinforcement: Read the social story with your child multiple times before the trip to reinforce understanding and familiarity.

- Customization: Tailor the story to your child's preferences, sensory sensitivities, and communication style.
- Review and Adjust: After the trip, review the social story with your child to discuss their experiences and make any necessary adjustments for future travels.

Incorporating social stories into your travel preparations can significantly enhance your child's comfort, confidence, and overall travel experience. They serve as a powerful tool to help your child navigate the complexities of travel while promoting a sense of security and understanding.

GPS and Tracking devices

Ensuring your child's safety when they are away is paramount. It's vital to establish a means of communication or a system to locate them if needed. For our sons, we've opted for child-friendly smartwatches. These watches not only allow us to be in touch but also permit them to reach out to us. Additionally, they incorporate GPS functionality, making it easier to track their whereabouts if, heaven forbid, they wander off. These watches are user-friendly and can include your contacts and reminders.

Here are some alternative GPS options for children with autism that you might consider. Please note that while I only have experience using the T-Mobile Timex Kids Watch, the following options were found online:

Here are some alternative GPS options for children with autism that you might consider:

AngelSense:

Designed specifically for children with special needs, AngelSense provides real-time tracking and alerts for location changes.

My Buddy Tag:

A wristband equipped with Bluetooth technology that alerts you if your child moves out of a set range.

Trax Play:

A small, lightweight GPS tracker that can be attached to clothing or accessories.

PocketFinder:

Offers GPS tracking and geofence alerts to notify you if your child goes beyond designated areas.

GizmoWatch:

Like a smartwatch, GizmoWatch offers two-way communication, GPS, and safety alerts.

T-Mobile Timex Kids Watch: This watch from T-Mobile provides GPS tracking, calling features, and customizable geofencing options.

Remember, each child is unique, so the choice of GPS product should align with your child's preferences and your family's needs. It's advisable to research and potentially consult with other parents who have used these devices before making a decision.

Schedules and Visuals

Schedules and visual aids play a critical role in supporting children with autism by providing structure, predictability, and improved communication. These tools help children better navigate their environment, understand routines, and express themselves effectively. Here's why schedules and visual aids are essential, along with detailed information about different types, obtaining them, and utilizing them effectively.

- **Predictability and Reduced Anxiety:** Children with autism often find comfort in routines. Schedules provide a visual representation of daily activities, reducing anxiety caused by unpredictability.
- **Enhanced Communication:** Visual aids offer an alternative means of communication for non-verbal or limited-verbal individuals, enabling them to express their needs, feelings, and thoughts.
- **Improved Understanding:** Visual cues help children comprehend abstract concepts and navigate complex information by breaking it down into manageable visual chunks.
- **Behavioral Regulation:** Schedules can help prevent behavioral challenges by indicating transitions and changes, minimizing frustration and meltdowns.
- **Increased Independence:** Visual supports empower children to carry out tasks independently, from dressing to completing daily routines.

Types of Schedules

Visual Schedules: Sequential images or icons depict the order of activities, enabling the child to anticipate and understand routines.

Written Schedules: Utilize written words to outline the day's events. These are beneficial for children who can read or are developing reading skills.

Object Schedules: Use actual objects to represent activities. For instance, a toothbrush signifies brushing teeth.

Types of Visuals

PECS (Picture Exchange Communication System): A system involving picture cards that the child can exchange to communicate their needs or desires.

Social Stories: Narrative-based visuals that explain situations, events, or expectations, helping the child comprehend and react appropriately.

Visual Cues: Single images representing a specific task or instruction, such as a picture of a bed to indicate bedtime.

AAC Devices vs Visual Aids

AAC Devices (Augmentative and Alternative Communication):

These are electronic devices that offer a range of communication methods, from symbol-based screens to synthesized speech. They are ideal for individuals with more complex communication needs.

Visual Aids: Visual supports encompass a broader range, including PECS, social stories, and visual cues. They can be simpler and are often used to enhance communication for individuals with varying abilities.

Obtaining Visuals

Online Resources: Websites like Boardmaker, Teachers Pay Teachers, and Autism Speaks offer a wide array of free and purchasable visual materials.

Creating Your Own: Use software like Microsoft Word or PowerPoint to design visuals tailored to your child's preferences and needs.

Using Visuals

Introduction: Introduce the visual aids and explain their purpose to the child.

Consistency: Use visuals consistently in daily routines to establish familiarity and understanding.

Teaching: Teach the child how to use each visual aid, whether it's exchanging a PECS card or referring to a visual schedule.

Communication: Encourage the child to use visuals to express their needs, preferences, and emotions.

Reinforcement: Praise and reward the child for using visuals effectively.

Schedules and visual aids are powerful tools that enhance communication, understanding, and independence for children with autism. By incorporating these tools into daily life, you can help your child thrive and navigate the world with greater confidence and ease.

Autism Glossary

- **504 Plan:** A legal document in the United States that outlines accommodations and modifications for students with disabilities to ensure their educational needs are met.
- **A-B-C Data:** Information collected to analyze the Antecedents, Behaviors, and Consequences of a particular behavior, often used in behavioral analysis.
- **Applied Behavior Analysis therapy (ABA):** a structured approach to improving socially significant behaviors in individuals with Autism Spectrum Disorder.
- **AAC Device:** Augmentative and Alternative Communication device, used to assist individuals with communication challenges in expressing themselves.
- **Apraxia:** A motor disorder that impairs an individual's ability to plan and execute coordinated movements, including speech.
- **Asperger's Syndrome:** A term previously used to describe a subtype of Autism Spectrum Disorder characterized by difficulties in social interaction and nonverbal communication, along with restricted and repetitive patterns of behavior.
- **Attention Deficit Disorder (ADD):** A condition characterized by difficulties in maintaining attention, often leading to distractibility and forgetfulness.

- **Attention Deficit Hyperactivity Disorder (ADHD):** A neurodevelopmental disorder marked by inattention, hyperactivity, and impulsivity.
- **Autism Spectrum Disorder (ASD):** A complex developmental disorder characterized by a range of challenges including difficulties in social interaction, communication, and restricted and repetitive behaviors.
- **BCAB Board Certified Assistant Behavior Analyst:** A professional who works under the supervision of a BCBA to implement behavior analysis interventions.
- **BCBA Board Certified Behavior Analyst:** A professional trained to analyze behavior and develop interventions based on Applied Behavior Analysis (ABA) principles.
- **BT Behavior Technician:** Is an individual who implements behavior interventions under the supervision of a BCBA.
- **Cognitive-Behavioral Therapy (CBT):** A therapeutic approach aimed at identifying and modifying negative thought patterns and behaviors.
- **DSM (Autism):** Diagnostic and Statistical Manual of Mental Disorders, a classification system used by mental health professionals to diagnose various mental disorders, including Autism Spectrum Disorder.
- **DSM-4:** The fourth edition of the Diagnostic and Statistical Manual of Mental Disorders, which provided diagnostic criteria for mental health conditions, including Autism Spectrum Disorder.
- **DSM-5:** The fifth edition of the Diagnostic and Statistical Manual of Mental Disorders, which provides updated criteria for diagnosing mental health conditions, including Autism Spectrum Disorder.

- **Echolalia:** The repetition of words or phrases, often seen in individuals with Autism Spectrum Disorder.
- **Elopement:** A term used to describe the act of leaving a safe environment without supervision, commonly seen in individuals with Autism Spectrum Disorder.
- **Executive Functioning:** Cognitive processes that help with organization, planning, decision-making, and controlling impulses.
- **Expressive Language:** The ability to express thoughts, feelings, and ideas through spoken language.
- **Fleeing:** A term used to describe sudden and purposeful movements away from a particular situation or environment, often observed in individuals with Autism Spectrum Disorder.
- **Gestalt Language:** A holistic and contextual approach to language comprehension and expression.
- **High Functioning Autism:** A term sometimes used to describe individuals with Autism Spectrum Disorder who exhibit milder symptoms and may have average to above-average intellectual abilities.
- **IEP:** Individualized Education Program, a personalized plan developed for students with disabilities to address their specific educational needs.
- **Inclusion:** The practice of integrating individuals with disabilities into mainstream environments, such as classrooms or social activities.
- **Joint Attention:** The ability to share focus on an object or topic with another person, often a challenge for individuals with Autism Spectrum Disorder.

- **LCSW:** Licensed Clinical Social Worker, a professional who provides mental health services, including therapy and counseling.
- **Level 1, Level 2, Level 3 Autism:** Categories that represent different levels of support needs in individuals with Autism Spectrum Disorder, with Level 1 requiring the least support and Level 3 requiring the most.
- **Low Functioning Autism:** A term sometimes used to describe individuals with Autism Spectrum Disorder who experience more severe symptoms and greater challenges in daily functioning.
- **Meltdowns:** Overwhelming responses to sensory or emotional stimuli, often resulting in emotional outbursts and loss of emotional regulation.
- **Non-Verbal:** A term used to describe individuals with Autism Spectrum Disorder who have limited or no verbal communication abilities.
- **Neurodivergent:** Refers to individuals whose neurological development and functioning differ from what is considered typical or "neurotypical."
- **Neurotypical:** Refers to individuals whose neurological development and functioning align with what is considered typical.
- **Occupational Therapist:** A healthcare professional who helps individuals develop or regain the skills needed for daily activities and tasks.
- **PEC Cards:** Picture Exchange Communication System cards, used to support nonverbal communication in individuals with Autism Spectrum Disorder.

- **Perseverate:** The repetition of a behavior, word, phrase, or thought, often seen in individuals with Autism Spectrum Disorder.

- **PICA:** The consumption of non-food substances, such as dirt or paper, often observed in individuals with Autism Spectrum Disorder.

- **Physical Therapist:** A healthcare professional who helps individuals improve their physical abilities and movement through exercises and interventions.

- **Play Therapy:** A therapeutic approach that uses play to help individuals with Autism Spectrum Disorder develop social, communication, and emotional skills.

- **Prosody:** The rhythm, intonation, and stress patterns in speech that convey emotional and contextual meaning.

- **Reinforcements**: Positive or negative consequences that follow a behavior and influence its likelihood of recurring.

- **Scripting:** The repetition of memorized phrases or lines from movies, books, or other sources, often seen in individuals with Autism Spectrum Disorder.

- **Self-Stimulatory Behavior:** Repetitive behaviors or movements, such as hand-flapping or rocking, often used by individuals with Autism Spectrum Disorder to self-soothe or regulate sensory input.

- **Sensory Diet:** A personalized plan of sensory activities and strategies designed to help individuals with sensory processing challenges regulate their sensory experiences.

- **Sensory Processing Disorder (SPD):** A condition in which the brain has difficulty processing and responding to sensory information from the environment.

- **Speech Therapist (SLP):** A healthcare professional who assesses and treats communication and speech disorders.

- **Stimming:** See "Self-Stimulatory Behavior (Stimming)."
- **Tantrums:** Intense emotional outbursts often seen in response to frustration or sensory overload.
- **Transition:** The process of moving from one life stage to another, often involving changes in routines and environments, which can be challenging for individuals with Autism Spectrum Disorder.
- **Triggers:** Stimuli or situations that can lead to emotional or behavioral reactions, often negatively affecting individuals with Autism Spectrum Disorder.

Admirable Professionals

Within the pages of the upcoming chapter, I am eager to share insights about highly recommended professionals in the field, along with individuals who possess a wealth of knowledge. Regardless of your location within the United States, I wholeheartedly encourage you to reach out to these exceptional people. Initiating contact with them allows you to express your concerns and inquire about any questions that may be on your mind.

These individuals and organizations have played a significant role in my personal journey with my son who has Autism. Through firsthand experience, I have witnessed their dedication, expertise, and genuine commitment to making a positive impact in the lives of children with Autism.

The inclusion of their details in this chapter is driven by my deep regard for their contributions. These are not just names on a page but individuals with whom I have collaborated closely, finding solace and guidance in their support. Their involvement has been instrumental in shaping my son's journey with Autism, and I am confident that their insights can be invaluable to others navigating similar paths.

As you explore this chapter, consider these connections as valuable resources. Whether you're seeking advice, professional guidance, or simply a supportive ear, these are individuals and organizations that have demonstrated a profound understanding of the challenges associated with Autism. Your proactive outreach to

98   Admirable Professionals

them could open doors to a network of support, encouraging a cooperative approach to addressing your concerns and questions.

In sharing this information, my hope is that you will find comfort, guidance, and a sense of community. Navigating the landscape of Autism can be complex, and the collective wisdom of these professionals can provide a compass for your own journey, promoting a collaborative approach to addressing your concerns and questions.

Eastside Therapy Services

Contact Info:

info@eastsidetherapyservices.com
P: (425) 459-5214

About our organization and what we offer:

Our approach at ETS focuses on a naturalistic and relationship based holistic skill building programs in pediatric therapy. Our specialty involves embedding pediatric therapy services within children's natural environments. We believe this builds meaningful skills in meaningful places which serves both children and their surrounding support system.

We serve as far North as Everett, as far South as Tukwila, and as far East as North Bend (and everywhere in between!). We work in many schools, early childhood programs, home's and community settings! Our team also operates our own naturalistic therapy center in Issaquah where we include further classroom and play based therapy options in addition to an animal therapy program (imagine the cutest of bunnies and the goofiest of goats!).

Our practice offers the following therapy services:

- Occupational Therapy
- Speech and Language Therapy
- Applied Behavior Analysis Therapy
- Comprehensive Autism Programs
- Feeding Therapy
- Parent Coaching
- Social Skills Group

Words of encouragement:

As we often say, there is no one like you or your child, and what a wonderful way to be! Neurodiversity is meaningful, complex, and something beautiful this world has included as long as it has existed. As parents to neurodiverse children, we get to know ourselves in new ways, know our children in new ways and have our perspectives and experiences shifted. It can also come with challenges and seeking support is an important step for many parents as they embark on their unique parenting journey. Celebration and love can co-exist with hard days, as all of us parents well know!

All parents need time, grace, learning and some trial and error. As we all know, just when we "get it figured out" our families and children's needs may change, and we start again! There is no one perfect answer that will work for all. The solutions, support, and resources you and your child will need will shift with time, age and circumstances and that is OK! We believe here that therapy should embrace who your child is while supporting them to build skills that bring them greater access to their world and values, and greater choice in their world. By embracing who someone is and offering support and care, we can teach one another to get to know and embrace exactly who we are as well. When seeking support for your child I encourage parents to find that balance of trusting your parent instincts, seeking understanding, and learning, and recognizing what values matter the most to your child and your family.

Speech For Success, PLLC

Contact Info:

contact@speechforsuccessllc.com

P: 425-405-0837

Services: Speech Therapy, Feeding Therapy and Occupational Therapy

About our organization and what we offer

At Speech for Success, we offer speech therapy, occupational therapy and feeding therapy for individuals in all ages and stages of life. All of our therapists have different passions and interests which have allowed us to service a large population of different people.

We are passionate about providing therapy support in a way that embraces neurodiversity. Our therapy approach will always start from a place of relationship with our clients and families.

Words of encouragement:

If you are a parent or caregiver with an Autistic child/family member, I know the world might look in and see someone who is "different" and make judgements. The best thing you can do for your loved one is first accept who they are in all of their neurological differences.

One of the things I have learned in my time as a therapist is I will not get ANYWHERE with my families or kids until I get into their world and make a connection. If this means my whole therapy session is dedicated to BIG movement, spinning or trapezing onto a crash mat, that is what I will do if it means I can see their joy! Once we can find connection, THEN I might start finding ways to support their communication. If I expect someone who sees and FEELS the world differently that I do, who am I to force them to communicate the way I do?

While I know it is hard to feel your loved one is looked at as "different", I believe strongly that is not the case. They have a mind that takes in the world completely in a different way than a neurotypical person and we as a society need to find ways to connect to how they are taking in this world, not forcing them to adapt to "one way" or "our way".

Your child/loved one is INCREDIBLE and has so many things to teach us. Let them shine in who they are and know you have support and people who want to help you on that journey.

Cindy Knighton, MS CCC-SLP

Ella: Occupational Therapist

My name is Ella and I am an occupational therapist working at Speech for Success. As an occupational therapist, I am often asked "what is Occupational Therapy? What do you do?"

Occupations refer to the meaningful activities that people do every day to occupy their time. Work, play, leisure, education, rest and sleep, and social participation are examples for "occupations". Occupational therapy helps people from any age to be functional and independent physically and mentally in their daily life, as well as to improve their quality of life.

As an Occupational therapist, my goal is to help kids to be successful at home and in school.

Areas Occupational Therapy focuses for children:

- Gross motor skills (running, jumping, doing stairs)
- Fine motor skills (handwriting, scissor)
- Emotional regulation
- Sensory regulation
- Feeding
- Self-care (dressing, potty training, using utensils)

Check out my OT blog at:

https://otellabella.wordpress.com for more OT information.

My advice for parents is You rock! You are amazing! You're not alone. Your child knows all the hard work and effort you as a parent does, even if they can't say it.

This world may be a challenging and unfamiliar world to children with Autism. Don't forget to praise, encourage, and trust them that they are strong enough to fight every challenge in life and be successful. Diagnosis can come with many fears and worries, but by the end of the day, the most important thing is for our kids to live happy lives. Please take a moment here to think about your child's strengths. What are their highlights?

Parents, please don't forget. Your child is a superstar, so are you!

Ella (Tzu-Yun) Wu

Lead Occupational Therapist, OTD, OTR/L

Columbia Virtual Academy

Contact Info: https://www.cva.org/

P: (855) 525-2270

About our organization and what we offer:

Columbia Virtual Academy is an accredited, tuition-free, K-12 alternative to traditional brick and mortar students that is available as public school for all residents of Washington State. We serve students from literally every corner of Washington State and everywhere in-between. Many students find their way to CVA that have not had great traditional brick and mortal school experiences. We offer both book and paper curriculums as well as a variety of online curriculums for our homeschool students. We offer a fully customizable education experience for every student and value the input of the primary teacher of each student (the parent/guardian) above all else. Parents, teachers and ideally students are involved in the creation, modification (as needed) and execution of the student's learning plan. This includes much more than choosing and sticking to a given curriculum. We can change or add curriculums and resources as needed, at any time. We also regularly (in coordination with families) modify learning activities to better fit student interests, needs and ability levels. If a student finishes a given curriculum, say 4 th grade level math, they can start into a 5th grade math curriculum of their choosing the very next school day. For many students with learning challenges, the opportunity to both receive a fully and continuously personalized educational experience while having the opportunity to make more than a year's worth of academic growth is very attractive.

Scott Huffman: Special Education Teacher

Words of encouragement:

I have had the opportunity to work with students on the spectrum in both traditional and home-school settings over the last fifteen years, and I have seen students on the spectrum succeed in both settings. At CVA, I've been lucky to work with many parents raising and educating neurodiverse students. I firmly believe that all kids deserve to be themselves, learn at their own pace, in their own way, while enjoying meaningful educational experiences. For many families, homeschooling, especially through CVA, allows just that. The benefits of homeschooling are many, especially for students on the spectrum. Many of the families I work with currently that have students on the spectrum report enjoying the opportunity to be flexible with their child's schedule, which can be helpful when scheduling around therapies, as well as controlling the schedule and sequencing of learning and customizing the learning activities. All students deserve an education that in customized to their strengths, needs and interests. I wish all my former, traditional school students could have the opportunity to have their learning be as customized or "just right" as my students at Columbia Virtual Academy do. It's an opportunity your child would have if homeschooled. However, I know it's a difficult decision to pull a student from a traditional school, and there are of course possible benefits as well as consequences to any action or inaction in life and as parents. I know for my two toddlers; I'm not yet decided on what is best for them or what their educational path will be. I know I will use a combination of the best available information, life experience and gut feeling to decide what is best for them. I hope this information helps you in that decision making process and wish nothing but the best for you and your children.

Taylor Spencer: General Education Teacher

Words of encouragement:

I have had the pleasure of being a part of Shae's sons' educational journey these past two years and look forward to many more. Seeing the progress made by her son in the past two years, and watching as he obtained his "twice-exceptional" designation last year, has been a highlight of my teaching career. I have taught in public schools in the state of Washington for 16 years. In my time in general education elementary classrooms, many things stood out to me as critical for the success of students.

Some of the areas include students that have strong family advocates willing to question the "norm" and learn about their child's educational needs, a team that believes in flexibility to address student needs, and educators and families willing to learn about neurodiversity through training, working with students, and learning how to best teach with respect to students' strengths. Working with students and learning how to best teach with respect to students' strengths. Working collaboratively in these ways provide a balanced learning plan and learning environment allows students to thrive. I am fortunate to work in an environment that believes in the same philosophies I do, Education should be asset-based, and neurodivergent students have various and incredible assets to offer! Finding programs that recognize your child's diverse needs as well as your child's strengths is incredibly important. We want our students to succeed in life, whatever that may look like for any individual. Part of success is creating a safe, nurturing environment that allows students to be themselves and strengthen their self-appreciation.

Shae has been a joy to work with, and I thoroughly enjoy getting to collaborate with her teacher to parents, and parent to parent. On a personal note, my toddler son is currently going through evaluation processes for ASD, and I have turned to Shae for advice on more than one occasion from the caregiver's perspective. Having a strong support system of caring individuals and not being afraid to reach out and create you "village" is necessary not only for surviva,l but for all of us to thrive.

My advice to all parents and educators: Advocate, empathize...you are all rock stars!

Taylor Spencer, NBCT, MS

K-8 Teacher, Columbia Virtual Academy

Katherine Blair: Psychologist

Words of encouragement:

I have enjoyed partnering with Shae as she navigates her son's world and educational needs. As a school psychologist, my role often involves sharing complex evaluation results that might seem daunting to parents. Through my experiences, I've learned that there is a delicate balance between explaining assessment scores for eligibility purposes and guiding teams through the intricate process of making recommendations for Individualized Education Programs (IEPs). Each child I work with is unique, and while there's no on-size-fits all approach, I've gathered some insights that I believe can benefit families in supporting their children's education. Firstly, I've found that understanding your child's rights lays a solid foundation for effective collaboration with their educational team. Open lines of communication with teachers, service providers, and administrators can greatly enhance the effectiveness of their program. Equipping yourself with knowledge about your child's strengths and needs also strengthens your ability to advocate on their behalf.

I also encourage parents to build a robust support network comprising teachers, therapists, doctors, and other professionals. Connecting with fellow parents who are also navigating the journey of raising children with special needs can offer invaluable mutual support and a wealth of shared information. Finally, success isn't always measured in standardized test scores; it manifests in various forms, unique to each child. Recognize and celebrating both major achievements and small victories on a daily basis is vital. Progress may sometimes seem slow, but maintaining a positive outlook is essential. Celebrating even the smallest milestones contributes significantly to your child's overall flourishing.

I appreciate the dedication Shae put into advocating for her son and many other children. Our partnership strives to meet her sons needs to benefit from this education.

Sincerely

Katherine Blair, Ed.S., NCSP

Dr. John Inman

Twice-Exceptional Children *Are* Gifts
Developing the Talents of 2e Children

"It is increasingly clear that when the educational focus is on talent and providing learning environments that align with the student's natural ways of learning, dramatic changes occur in motivation, self-esteem, and behavior."
Susan Baum & Steven Owen

What if you could explore twice-exceptionality through the eyes of a researcher who grew up and lived as a 2e person? And what if the lived experience told, is backed by extensive research? I am this person. I tell my story through the lens of a researched-based autoethnography, focusing on my own journey to understand and heal, on others who are experiencing what I experienced, and on the larger societal impact of twice-exceptional children who lack the nurturing to develop their talents. There is a lifelong impact of growing up being told I was broken and in need of fixing. I imagine what my lived experience might have been like had I grown up in a traditional Indigenous learning environment where all talents are recognized as gifts. Join me on this journey and discover the gift of 2e.

Dr. Inman has been blessed with both gifted and deficit exceptionalities. He grew up believing he was broken and in need of fixing, a frame of mind that has haunted him his whole life. He did not realize he had gifts until conducting research for his doctorate in education. Rather than just experience the impact of being 2e, Dr. Inman decided to do something about the experience other children have growing up feeling broken and in need of fixing. His book is the outcome of that mission. With extensive experience and a deep understanding of how humans organize into communities, communicate through dialogue to create meaningful and lasting change, and how humans of all ages learn, grow, and contribute to the world, he helps educators collaborate to craft unique paths forward to transform how children and adults learn together.

www.learningexceptionalities.com

Sana Tariq

Director of Special Education

Sana Tariq is an impassioned education leader and seasoned systems builder, amassing over a decade of experience dedicated to steering strategic initiatives that not only maximize equitable access and inclusion but also underscore the importance of having an Individualized Education Program (IEP) advocate. With a proven track record in leading multifaceted special education programs, Sana ensures strict adherence to the Individuals with Disabilities Education Act (IDEA) and Free Appropriate Public Education (FAPE) guidelines while actively promoting culturally responsive frameworks.

Her commitment extends beyond the administrative landscape into the vital realm of advocacy for families and children navigating the complex intricacies of school systems, particularly those with special needs. Functioning as an IEP advocate, Sana stands as a staunch ally for families, utilizing her wealth of information to empower them with a comprehensive understanding of their rights within the IEP process.

The significance of having an IEP advocate cannot be overstated. In the labyrinth of educational policies, an advocate like Sana acts as a knowledgeable guide, offering invaluable support to families by interpreting and elucidating the intricacies of the IEP. They bridge the gap between educational jargon and a family's understanding, ensuring that parents are well-informed advocates for their children. In essence, an IEP advocate such as Sana becomes a catalyst for fostering collaboration, facilitating communication between educators, parents, and the school system, ultimately working towards the shared goal of providing the best possible educational experience for children with special needs.

For those seeking guidance or interested in connecting with Sana, she can be reached on her website: equityineducation.net

Learning To Play

Learning to Play (LTP) serves children, families, and the community by providing virtual support, digital guides, in-person play and social skills groups using behavior analytic principles through a social-emotional lens. Our families may be seeking support with autism, an autism diagnosis, school transitions, social skills, sibling relationships, challenging behavior, or simply creating routines at home. We prioritize meeting families where they are at, building strong emotional foundations for learning, and respecting diverse cultural backgrounds. Through customized, family-driven goals, we aim to enhance parent-child relationships and share our knowledge with the community through outreach and continuous learning about autism and advocacy.

Adriana Luna, Ph.D., BCBA-D, LBA

Co-founder

Adriana is originally from California and moved to Seattle in 2016. Being bilingual in Spanish and English, Adriana is passionate about working with Spanish-speaking families. Adriana received her PhD in Special Education from the University of Washington in 2023 and is currently a postdoctoral research fellow. When she is not working with her colleagues at UW or LTP, Adriana likes to enjoy time with her husband, friends, her feisty cat named Patches, or her cozy pup named Theo.

Mika Aoyama, M.Ed., BCBA, LBA

Mika is Seattle native and graduated from Gonzaga University (Go Zags!). She began her teaching career in Fort Collins, Colorado as an Early Childhood Special Education Teacher. After returning to Seattle to pursue a graduate degree at the University of Washington, Mika graduated in 2017 with a Masters in Special Education and Applied Behavioral Analysis. Mika enjoys spending time with her husband, family, baking sourdough bread, and having picnics at the beach.

Admirable Professionals

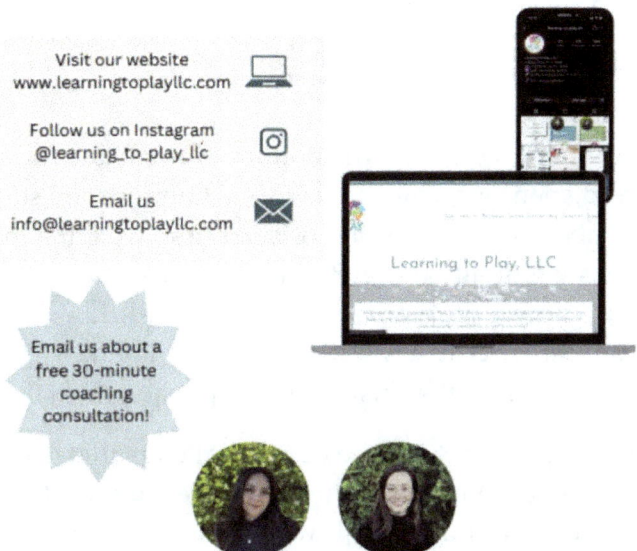

Adriana Luna and Mika Fernandez are co-owners of Learning to Play, LLC. Learning to Play (LTP) was started in 2021 and is dedicated to empowering parents and caregivers with the tools and knowledge to help each family thrive. Adriana and Mika specialize in virtual parent coaching and inclusive playgroups in the Seattle, WA area.

Words from the Author

I want to thank you from the bottom of my heart for picking up my book and spending your time with it. Our journey started when we learned about our son's diagnosis. At first, we felt a mix of relief and worry as we finally understood why our son acted the way he did. But deep down, we were scared that we wouldn't know how to help him properly because we didn't know enough. As parents, we felt a strong determination inside us that pushed us to fight for him.

With a strong spirit, we faced every challenge that came our way, even when things looked tough. We proved the odds wrong and achieved things we didn't think were possible for our son. It took almost three years to build a team of people to help our son— therapists, teachers, doctors, family, and friends who care. We know that not everyone has this kind of support, and that's why I wrote this book. My hope is that it can ease some of the stress and worry you might have on your own journey.

Let's be real, this journey won't be easy. There will be days when everything seems hard and dark. But remember this, don't stop moving forward. Keep pushing on, keep fighting. You'll find a strength inside you that comes from love, and you'll see your child achieve things that will make you proud. Keep fighting because you are a warrior who can't be stopped.

These little angels came into the world without knowing how complicated it can be. It's up to us to make a world where they feel loved and strong. So, just keep fighting, and remember, you're never alone in this.

Fighting alongside with you, your fellow soldier in solidarity

Shae

www.ingramcontent.com/pod-product-compliance
Lightning Source LLC
LaVergne TN
LVHW021943060526
838200LV00042B/1906